steps, while also digging to the roots of the problem, beneath the pile of clothes, the stack of shoes, and the mountain of frustration. I nodded my head in agreement from cover to cover. I think you will too."

—Melissa Coleman, author of *The Minimalist Kitchen*

"If you're thinking about optimizing your wardrobe, let Courtney Carver be your guide. She will show you how to let go of excess stuff so that you can bring more joy, gratitude, and love into your life. As Courtney says, 'Simplicity is the way back to love,' and this book is full of loving advice and stories. I highly recommend *Project 333*!"

—Tammy Strobel, author, photographer, and founder of RowdyKittens.com

"For me, Project 333 became something far greater than wearing fewer articles of clothing. It became about recognizing the value of boundaries. And the value of boundaries reaches far beyond our closets. It begins to spill into how we decorate our homes, the toys we buy for our children, and even how we choose to spend our time, money, and energy. This book is a must-read for those who are ready to simplify their lives."

—Joshua Becker, author of
The Minimalist Home and *The More of Less*

"Project 333 is not just a fashion challenge, it's an invitation to live more intentionally. Courtney takes a gentle, heart-based approach to decluttering and provides readers with plenty of support along the way."

—Francine Jay, author of *The Joy of Less* and *Lightly*

"Courtney Carver understands the unstoppable power of less."

—Joshua Fields Millburn, cofounder of *The Minimalists*

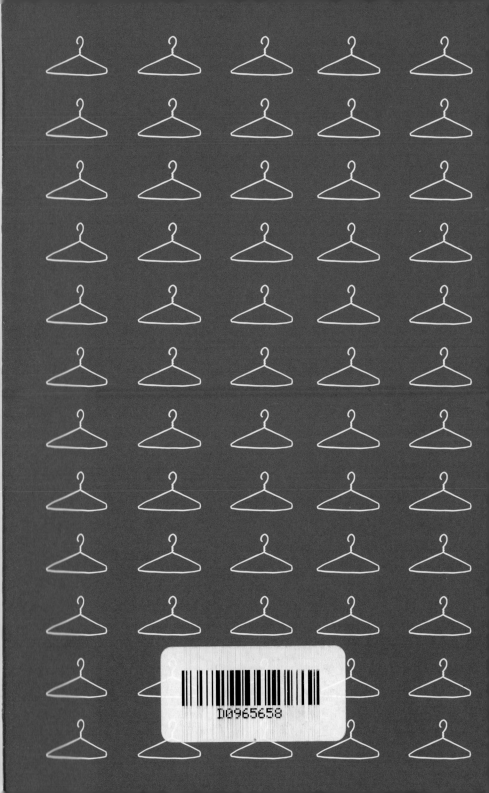

"Courtney does an extraordinary job helping us address the physi
and emotional clutter that comes with our wardrobe."

—Ryan Nicodemus, cofounder of *The Minimali*

"For me, the key to making life simple again started in my closet wi
Project 333. I've learned to not let the things I wear, wear me out. I'
dressing with less, and feeling twice as confident. And for that I'
truly grateful. Allow yourself the possibility of life transformation b
simply starting with your wardrobe."

—Angel Chernoff, *New York Times* bestselling author o
Getting Back to Happy and 1000+ *Little Things*

"I opened *Project 333* thinking I could use some help scaling down my
closet. Little did I know this practical guidebook would lead me to
uncover a major source of stress in my life. Within days of practicing
the principles in *Project 333*, I began seeing my life's clutter and excess
for what they really were—unnecessary burdens that have weighed
me down for decades and distracted me from what really matters.
With wisdom, humor, compassion, and practicality, Courtney Carver
teaches us to notice what's actually serving the life around us so we
can begin making sound emotional and financial choices for ourselves
and those we love. Because of *Project 333*, my family is discovering
unlimited possibilities created by living lighter and happier with less!"

—Rachel Macy Stafford, *New York Times* bestselling author of
Hands Free Mama; Hands Free Life; and *Only Love Today*

"I've come to believe that simplicity, in its final form, always looks so
simple and easy, but getting there is always hard. In *Project 333*,
Courtney guides you toward simplicity in your closet with doable

project 333

project 333

THE MINIMALIST
FASHION CHALLENGE
THAT PROVES LESS REALLY
IS SO MUCH MORE

Courtney Carver

A TARCHERPERIGEE BOOK

tarcherperigee

an imprint of Penguin Random House LLC
penguinrandomhouse.com

Most TarcherPerigee books are available at special quantity discounts for bulk
purchase for sales promotions, premiums, fund-raising, and educational needs.
Special books or book excerpts also can be created to fit specific needs. For details,
write: SpecialMarkets@penguinrandomhouse.com.

Library of Congress Cataloging-in-Publication Data

Names: Carver, Courtney, author.
Title: Project 333 : the minimalist fashion challenge that proves less really
   is so much more / Courtney Carver.
Other titles: Project three hundred thirty-three
Description: New York: TarcherPerigee, 2020. | "A TarcherPerigee book."
Identifiers: LCCN 2019027100 | ISBN 9780525541455 (hardcover) |
   ISBN 9780525541462 (ebook)
Subjects: LCSH: Clothing and dress—Psychological aspects. | Simplicity. |
   Minimal design. | Self-realization.
Classification: LCC GT524 .C37 2020 | DDC 391—dc23
LC record available at https://lccn.loc.gov/2019027100

Printed in the United States of America
10 9 8 7 6 5 4 3 2 1

Book design by Lorie Pagnozzi
Illustrations by Emma Block

For every brave, curious heart willing
to ask, "Wouldn't it be crazy if . . ."

CONTENTS

project 333

333

WHEN I CREATED THE MINIMALIST FASHION CHALLENGE Project 333 in 2010, I wasn't interested in creating a capsule wardrobe. I didn't want to develop a personal style. (I thought that was a lost cause.) In fact, my motives had very little to do with clothes. I just wanted some peace. I wanted a break from the excess. I wanted relief from running late in the morning after trying on several outfits. I wanted to feel good in my clothes. I wanted to stop obsessing over what I was going to wear to work, to dinner, or to an event.

I wanted to stop feeling like I didn't have enough . . . like I wasn't enough.

The average woman owns $550 in clothing that has never been worn. We wear 20 percent of our clothing 80 percent of the time, yet 100 percent of our wardrobe gets 100 percent of our attention, emotion, space, and time. That's exhausting.

Don't you want some relief . . . a little peace?

Organizing your closet year after year or season after

season is just a Band-Aid for a much larger problem. We have too much. We have way more than we need and have been led to believe that we still don't have enough. We don't have the right shoes, the trendy coat for the season, the perfect little black dress, or the latest and greatest handbag. Between constant comparing, attractive advertising campaigns, and ridiculously low fast-fashion prices, we just add, and add, and add. And it's never enough.

WHAT IS PROJECT 333?

Project 333 is an invitation to create space in your closet, time in your life, and love in your heart. It's a call for less and a chance to completely redefine your relationship with stuff and shopping, especially the stuff you put on your body every day. Project 333 is an opportunity to think differently, dress differently, and learn about what you really want and need in your closet and in your life.

ALL RIGHT, BUT WHAT IS IT REALLY?

Okay . . . here it is. Project 333 is a minimalist fashion challenge where you dress with only 33 items—including clothing, accessories, jewelry, and shoes—for 3 months. I'm going to tell you more about the rules later on, but right now, you're probably either thinking, *Cool . . . let's do it*, or . . . *That's nice, but not for me*. Or . . . *You crazy*. Most people don't fall anywhere in the middle. They're either all in or all out. At first. What I'm trying to say is, don't worry about your immediate reaction. By the time you're done reading this book, you'll have a better idea of what to expect and how this little challenge might change your closet and your entire life.

HOW IT GOT STARTED

I started this challenge as a personal experiment in 2010 because my closet was completely out of control. I had been collecting clothes (and other stuff, as we do) for decades. When my closet got too full, I'd put things in boxes, drawers, or other closets to spread it all out. I'd do the spring cleaning thing and the "new year, new you" thing and lighten up a bit. Eventually, though, I'd fill up the space. I always needed something new in my closet for a new season or a new event, and often for emotional reasons. Shopping made me feel better. Not for long, but for a minute, at least.

Before I created the rules for Project 333, I looked for a challenge online. I had been simplifying my life for several years, slowly and gently, but I knew my slow-and-steady approach to change wouldn't work for my closet. I had long passed the opportunity for slow-and-steady change with my clothes. I needed to change the inside of my closet, but I also needed to change the way I thought about my clothes, closet, and shopping habits. I couldn't find the challenge I was looking for, so I made it. On October 1, 2010, I promised myself (and the internet) that I would dress with less (way less than I was used to) for three months. I didn't know what to expect. I didn't have any specific goals. Like I said, I really just wanted some peace. Thinking about what to wear, what to buy, what to keep, what to donate, what to sell, and what looked good was exhausting. Trying on outfits, worrying about what people would think, and taking care of my big wardrobe had taken over such a big part of my life, and I was over it. I'd been shopping my whole life, and I still had nothing to wear.

When I started the challenge, I was working full-time in advertising sales (oh, the irony) for a group of magazines. I remember looking at the tiny capsule wardrobe I had created and thinking, *This won't be enough*, and *People will notice*, and *Is this crazy?* My work life was back-to-back meetings and events, and my real life (I never considered my work as "real life" because I wanted out so badly) consisted of taking care of my family, hiking, date nights, hanging out with friends . . . and shopping. I was worried, but I knew it was time to change anyway. If I didn't change, nothing would change.

WHAT PROJECT 333 ISN'T

- It's not a *what to wear* or *what not to wear* wardrobe formula. People have created Project 333 capsule collections from 33 black items, 33 very colorful patterned items, and everything in between. While you'll see some different examples throughout the book, the beauty of the challenge is that you get to wear *your* favorite clothes every day.
- It's not a competition. Even though you'll experience lots of personal wins, there is no winner of Project 333. In this challenge and community, we don't compete with each other,

but instead support each other. We lift each other up and inspire by sharing what we are wearing, what we are learning, and how we are growing.

- It's not an exact science. I chose the number 33 based on a list of items I made anticipating what I thought I would need for 3 months. The list had about 45 items on it, but since this is a challenge, I chose 33. I wasn't sure if it would work, but I liked the sound of 33 items for 3 months, 333. I recommend starting with 33, but your number might be different. We'll dig into that later.

- It's not a project in suffering. One afternoon I was waiting for a train with my daughter in NYC. I was wearing a blue-and-white-striped shirt, one of my 33 items. When I took a sip of my coffee, it dribbled out of the badly sealed lid and landed all over my shirt. After a good laugh, I went in search of a new shirt. I wasn't going to wear the stained shirt all day in the name of simplicity or to comply with the challenge rules of not buying new things. If something you included in your 33 items gets ripped or stained, or no longer fits at some point, there is no need to suffer through it. Replace or mend the item and move on.

FIVE THINGS YOU'LL GAIN BY DRESSING WITH LESS

There are many reasons to try Project 333. While you can expect your own individual experience and benefits, here are a few things that most people gain as a result of dressing with less and trying this closet challenge.

MONEY: A commitment to Project 333 isn't just a commitment to dress with less; it's also an invitation to call a full stop to shopping for three months. Even if you don't think you spend much on shoes, clothing, accessories, or jewelry, you may be surprised how those (big and little) purchases add up.

TIME: Think about how much time you spent last month shopping in stores or online. How much time did you spend weeding through emails with special offers or trying on different outfits from your current collection? And the time you spent getting ready every morning? Now add the time you spent thinking about a past or future purchase. For the next three months, you get all that time back.

SPACE: Even though you won't get rid of the excess stuff right away, it will be out of sight. You'll gain physical space in your immediate surroundings and mental space by clearing out the clutter.

CLARITY: Once you've selected your 33 items, you don't have to think much about what to wear for the next three months. You won't have to worry about what's on sale, what you need to buy, or what's missing from your closet. By reducing those decisions, you can consider what really matters to you and have more clarity throughout the day. Bye-bye, decision fatigue.

FREEDOM: A closet full of clothes that don't fit, things you paid too much for, and items you don't wear weigh on you every time you're looking for something to wear. Opening my closet used to be a daily reminder of my debt and discontent. There were the clothes that didn't fit, the clothes I never wore, and even clothes with price tags still hanging from them. Once the excess went out the door, so did the guilt and other emotions I had been paying with for so long. When I let go, I realized I had paid enough. I had paid with my money, my time, my attention, and my emotions. Haven't you paid enough, too? With only your favorite things hanging in your closet, you'll experience freedom from the guilt and weight of the excess items you currently face every morning.

COURTNEY'S FIRST 333

Before I take you down this path of life-changing closet reconstruction, I should probably tell you who I am (the very short version). First, I'm married to the love of my life, and mom to a twentysomething daughter who also happens to be my favorite person. Next, I'm an author, blogger, speaker, creative, and introvert. I spent many years working in sales, marketing, and advertising, but after being diagnosed with multiple sclerosis in 2006, I released the majority of the stress from my life (including getting rid of my clutter, debt, and house) and left my secure career path to do work that makes me smile. I have a blog, bemorewithless.com, which most people discover after googling Project 333. I wrote a book called *Soulful Simplicity* to share my story and included a short chapter about Project 333.

Now I've written this entire book about Project 333, including a short paragraph about my story. That's usually how it goes when I mention Project 333—it takes over the conversation!

I'm going to tell you much more about how I did it, how you can do it, what obstacles I faced, and how other people are changing their closets and lives with Project 333, but here's a quick breakdown of what I included in my first collection (the detailed list is at https://bemorewithless.com/minimalist-fashion -project-333-begins):

- 21 ARTICLES OF CLOTHING
- 6 ACCESSORIES
- 2 PIECES OF JEWELRY
- 4 PAIRS OF SHOES

My 33-item collections have changed and evolved over time, but I usually end up with a similar category breakdown. In the beginning, the simplicity factor was only limiting the number of items in my wardrobe, but now I apply a lens of simplicity to the individual items I include, too. Is it easy to care for? Does it play well with others? Does it fit my body and my lifestyle, maybe even many facets of my lifestyle? Keep reading to find out how to build your own capsule collection for the challenge and why it matters. I'll make suggestions about what to include, and tell you what you don't have to count in your 33, too.

For many years, I bought into the idea that there was a perfect little black dress for me. I was sure a new scarf would complete a look, and maybe even complete me. I thought those shoes (that I could barely walk in) made me look powerful. What I didn't know before I tried three months of dressing with less was that I am not what I wear. People don't care what I'm wearing. And, most important, I need way less than I think I do to be happy. Simple is the new black.

MORE

IF YOU'RE READING THIS BOOK HOPING FOR A recommendation for the perfect pair of jeans or a little black dress that you don't want to live without, do a quick review of your wardrobe history. How many pairs of jeans have you owned in your lifetime? How many little black dresses? How many stylish bags? How is that working for you?

The truth is, there will never be an item of clothing that changes your life or convinces people you are someone you are not. Shopping won't fix the past or secure the future. More is not the answer. Before I discovered the power of less, reduced stress, and simplified my life, I thought the answer to all my problems was more. I thought I would be happier with more money, more closet space, more shopping, more spending, and more stuff overall. I thought people would like/love/respect me more if I did more for them, and proved myself by doing more in every area of my life. But more, more, more didn't result in more happiness, closer relationships, or better health. It did the opposite. My quest for more resulted in stress, depression, and strained relationships, and it eventually led to exhaustion and illness.

My favorite place for more was my closet. If I gained weight, I bought more clothing. If I lost weight, I bought more clothing. If nothing seemed to fit, I bought more shoes instead. If I had an upcoming event, I bought more clothes, and more accessories to dress up the clothes. If I had a good day, I'd celebrate with a shopping trip. If I found a shirt I liked, I bought more of them, in different colors (and then wore the black one all the time). If I had a bad day, I'd medicate with more shopping. Seeking more was one way to go, but it wasn't a good one, because it contributed to my sense of discontent. Something wasn't right, but I didn't know what it was. Instead of trying to figure it out, I turned to more; more stuff, more busyness, more shopping. When things are broken but bearable, it feels easier at first to stay at "bearable" rather than address the problems.

As I began to let go of things in an effort to reduce stress, I felt something I hadn't felt in many years. I felt light. I also began to feel happier and healthier, so I kept going. Soon enough, less replaced more as a new direction and solution that I hadn't expected. Less was the answer. I noticed that when I had less to take care of, worry about, and think about . . . I felt lighter. I removed things from my diet, my calendar, and my budget. Then it was time to consider my stuff. At first I didn't think my stuff, the clutter I had collected for decades, was stressful, but eventually I realized it was. It weighed me down and kept me distracted. Once I saw the stuff as stress, I wanted to give it all away. Luckily, I didn't (otherwise this might be called Project 33 instead of 333). At first I back-burnered the "more" in my closet because I didn't want to go there. I had some pretty solid reasons for holding on to the stuff in my closet. After all, I had spent a lot of money buying it all, and some of it had sentimental value; I also thought people judged me on what I was wearing. I had all kinds of identity issues and emotions tied up in my wardrobe, so it was hard to think about. I worked on simplifying other things first and then decided it was time to go into my closet and start Project 333.

MORE OF THE GOOD STUFF: WHAT TO EXPECT FROM PROJECT 333

There's one thing you should know right away. You don't have to get rid of all the "more" in your closet when you start Project 333. In fact, I don't recommend that you do. All I ask is that you hide the extra stuff. Get everything out of sight when you start the challenge. There's a method to my madness here. The separation you create will matter later. It will make it easier to identify what you enjoy wearing and what needs to go. The distance you put between you and your excess stuff will make it easier to let go, too. You simply won't care about it like you did when you had to look at it every day when you opened your closet. I remember going into my boxes of stored items after my first three months with 33 items, and my first thought when looking through everything was, *What was I thinking?* Why had I held on for so long to pieces that I didn't enjoy and never wore? Why did I spend so much time feeling bad about not wearing them? A few months apart, and all I could think was, *Time to donate this stuff.* Even though all the extra stuff eventually went out the door, if I had let go of it immediately, I would have wondered if I had made the right decision and worried that I would have to buy everything again, creating extra stress. Take this part of the challenge more cautiously, and instead of letting go right away of all the excess stuff, fake it by getting it out of sight for three months.

Even though less replaced more as my go-to problem-solving technique, I can't help but celebrate the kind of more that has come from dressing with less. Everyone experiences this a little differently, but this is what I've heard from people who try Project 333.

"I HAVE MORE TIME IN THE MORNING." This is usually the first benefit people notice when they take the challenge. Instead of spending time trying on different outfits or stressing about what to wear, they have time for breakfast, meditation, or starting the day at a slower, more peaceful pace.

"I'M SAVING MORE MONEY." No doubt about this one. I took my weekly shopping trips to quarterly or even less frequently with Project 333.

"I HAVE MORE ATTENTION FOR WHAT INTERESTS ME." Imagine if we harnessed all the energy and attention we spend on how we look and what we wear and instead directed it toward things that really matter to us and to the world.

"I GET MORE COMPLIMENTS." This one was a surprise. I started to receive not only more compliments, but different compliments. Instead of "I like that necklace/those shoes," I heard more things like, "You look so good" or "What is it about you that's changed? You look great."

"I HAVE MORE CONFIDENCE." This was just one of many inside shifts. I had given so much power to my clothes, I forgot that confidence comes from the inside.

These weren't the only changes. People who tried Project 333 noticed less anxiety and more clarity and focus. They reported they had more patience with their children and that they were sleeping better. The shifts that were happening in my life, and that I was hearing about from others, had nothing to do with shirts, shoes, scarves, or belts. The changes we noticed were heart-shifts.

YOU HAVE TO START SOMEWHERE

Minimalist fashion challenge Project 333 isn't about fashion or clothes, but that's where it starts. When you realize how much stress you can release, how much space you can create, how much money you can save, and how much joy you will experience simply by reducing the number of items in your closet, you'll wonder why you didn't start sooner. This challenge begins with a focus on less in the form of fewer items in your wardrobe, but the results and insights you'll glean will have very little to do with what's on your hangers. Instead, they'll be focused on more of the good stuff, more proof that less is, in fact, so much more. If more isn't working for you either, try less.

EMOTION

sad, mad, guilty, or frustrated? I had no idea how much emotion
my clothes held until I let them go. I had no idea that the clothes
in my closet were stressful. I knew there was stress in the way I
managed money (not well), and that stress was in my schedule,
job, and relationships, but my wardrobe? I actually thought my
clothes and, more specifically, my shopping for clothes were a
stress reliever. When I wanted to escape a crappy workday, or
disappointing news, or my sheer exhaustion from doing life,
shopping soothed me. I looked forward to the promise of something new to lift me up and make me feel better. I had an emotional connection to the individual items in my closet, too.
There were the pair of shoes that cut off circulation to my toes,
but because I had spent so much hard-earned money on them,
I had to wear them. And the jeans that barely fit me in college
that I knew I could squeeze into again one day if I could just
lose a few pounds. I had the fancy scarves, too, that I never

knew how to tie, but believed could bring me to a new level of sophistication if I could figure them out. The funny thing is that all the items I purchased to feel better only made me feel worse.

I rarely shopped because I needed new clothes, but instead shopped to feel better, to relieve the pain of boredom and working a job I didn't enjoy, and because I honestly believed that something new would make me happier or improve my life in some way. I was emotional about how I shopped and about what I owned. If someone gave me something as a gift and I couldn't see myself wearing it, I still hung it in my closet as a demonstration of love and respect and felt bad later for never wearing it. Or when I finally felt ready to let go of something, I'd feel guilty because I had spent so much money on, or invested so much energy in, something I never wore. There was also the negativity that came from holding on to pieces that didn't fit me. I usually had (at least) two sizes of clothes in my closet, the ones that fit me and the ones I wished would fit me. Combine that with my very high propensity for sentimentality, and it makes sense that my closet was packed not just with clothes but with feelings and emotions, too.

LET'S UNPACK THE EMOTIONS . . .

- GUILT: You may feel guilty for spending too much, for not wearing things you spent too much on, for the price tags still hanging on several items, or because you give too much attention to your wardrobe. Guilt may come from not fitting into clothes that used to fit you or not fitting into clothes that never fit you to begin with. It's utter madness what we do to ourselves while simply getting dressed.

- FRUSTRATION: Nothing fits, nothing looks good. That "oh shit" moment when you look around and everything you thought you liked is on the floor because you definitely can't wear it today. Typically, I've found this emotion has nothing to do with my clothes and everything to do with something completely unrelated. Now if I'm frustrated with my clothes, I take a step back, reflect, and address what's really frustrating me. For instance, if I had disappointing news earlier in the day, or I'm hungry or tired, I can't see it right away and blame my wardrobe instead.

- SADNESS: Seeing the outfit you wore to an event that made you sad will make you sad. Holding on to your ex's sweatshirt or your old work uniform can make you sad. Keeping a loved one's clothes in your closet after they die is rarely comforting. You don't get to hold on to people, relationships, or any part of the past just because you are holding on to the stuff.

Typically we don't feel these negative emotions until we open the closet doors. Seeing the clothes triggers the emotions. And the really destructive part is that until we are clued in and paying attention, we don't know why we feel a little shitty after getting dressed. It becomes so everyday, so normal, that we just accept it. We accept it, ignore it, and carry the weight around from day to day, month to month, and year to year. Unintentionally, we punish ourselves and we don't even know why. If facing those emotions and punishing yourself is not how you want to start your day, let go of the emotions by letting go of the items that trigger them.

If you want to be free of these painful emotions right away, let go of . . .

CLOTHES THAT DON'T FIT YOUR BODY TODAY. Hide all the items that don't fit. Too small? Too big? Either way, get it out. Even if you struggle with weight fluctuation, give yourself a break. Your too-small clothes aren't making you smaller, and your too-big clothes aren't making you bigger. See what happens when you accept the person you are and the body you have today, and dress for that. If that changes, change your clothes.

CLOTHES SOMEONE GAVE YOU THAT YOU NEVER WEAR. Accept the gift with the intention it was given and then move on. If it's something you would never wear, pass it on. And P.S.—as grown adults, let's stop buying clothes for each other, okay?

CLOTHES THAT DON'T FIT YOUR LIFESTYLE. Are you holding on to clothes you wore for a prior life or for a life you aspire to have? Dress for the life you have right now, and you will move through it with more ease and grace.

CLOTHES YOU COULD NOT AFFORD. If you don't let go now, you will pay again and again and again. You have paid enough.

CLOTHES THAT MAKE YOU FEEL SAD OR BAD. If there are items in your closet that are dragging you down because they remind you of a sad occasion or a bad time, or because they make you feel like you aren't good enough in any way, know that you are allowing that to happen. You get what you accept. Give up the items, and you give up the negative emotions, too.

STUFF AND SHOPPING WON'T MAKE YOU FEEL BETTER

When you're feeling all the feelings, your body isn't saying, "Hey, let's go shopping." It's saying, "Please take care of me." If we take the time to pay attention to what our hearts are really screaming for, we know it's not a trip to the mall or our favorite place to shop online. Even though it often feels like a quick fix, it won't last and leads only to more guilt, anger, and frustration. Instead, trade the quick fixes for true healing and self-care. Here are a few examples of where to start:

- TAKE A BATH
- GO FOREST BATHING OR TAKE A LONG WALK
- HAVE A SOLO DANCE PARTY

- GO FOR A FACIAL OR TURN YOUR HOME INTO A MINI RETREAT WITH CANDLES, A FACE MASK, AND RELAXING MUSIC
- CALL SOMEONE WHO MAKES YOU LAUGH EVEN WHEN YOU'RE DOWN
- WRITE A LETTER TO YOUR YOUNGER SELF OR OLDER SELF
- HELP SOMEONE ELSE
- SLEEP IN

Use these techniques anytime (even if you aren't feeling bad) to build some resilience for the tough days. Marketers and advertisements want us to believe that they have the cure for what ails us, but if we're willing to get still for a minute, we can tap in to our own heart's calling and healing. We know what we need most if we're willing to listen to and trust our hearts. You may not recognize the emotions you face on a daily basis until the stuff is gone. And then, when you have a little space to bathe in the relief you feel, you'll start to remember who you are.

ECO

I DIDN'T START PROJECT 333 FOR THE ECO BENEFITS, but there are plenty. Dressing with less isn't just good for you— it's good for the planet, too. While there are many things you can do and consider, simply dressing with less and reducing your footprint by consuming less are big eco-friendly steps in the right direction. Consider these Sustainable Fashion Facts from Shannon Lohr (@factory45co on Instagram). Shannon is an entrepreneur and founder of Factory45, an online accelerator program that takes sustainable fashion companies from idea to launch. She's also my friend and go-to expert on all things eco-friendly fashion.

- The world now consumes about 80 billion new pieces of clothing every year.
- Ninety-five percent of discarded clothing can be recycled or upcycled.

- The amount of water used in apparel production each year is enough to fill 32 million Olympic-size swimming pools. Meanwhile, 1.1 billion people lack access to safe drinking water.
- A $25 T-shirt would be only $1.35 more expensive if the wages of the worker who made it were doubled.
- By extending the life of your clothing by an additional nine months, you can reduce your carbon, water, and waste footprints by 20 to 30 percent each.
- Clothing made from conventional polyester can take up to two hundred years to decompose in a landfill.
- Making a pair of jeans uses the same amount of water as flushing your toilet for three years.
- The average American woman wears just 20 percent of her wardrobe.

The average annual clothing consumption per person in the US is sixty-five garments, according to the American Apparel & Footwear Association. That's an entirely new wardrobe every year. Do we need a new wardrobe every year? In the beginning, I didn't give much thought to these statistics or to how my consumption behaviors were contributing to anything or anyone besides myself. Shopping made me feel better, so researching things that made me feel bad about the behavior that made me feel good wasn't an option. At first.

(Side note: Sometimes, when people hear about the Project 333 "33 items for 3 months" rule, they assume that means

33 different or new items every three months. Noooooooooo. I'll tell you more about this later, but our intention here is to reduce our consumption and reduce the overall size of our wardrobes.)

Before I could learn about the dark side of fashion, I had to find better ways to take care of myself. Once I realized that my shopping trips and new items weren't making me feel better for very long anyway, it was almost easy to replace them with other ways of taking care of myself when I didn't feel well, or when I was bored, frustrated, or feeling any of a million other emotions. The purpose of the shift wasn't to feel fewer emotions or to feel them less deeply, only to find a better way to address them. It's amazing how much a walk in the woods (or a nap, or a drink of water) can do for your soul. Often, the solution to our pain is much smaller than we think. Author Glennon Doyle says, "I tend toward dramatic thinking. When I have a problem or when I feel icky, I tend to think the solution is: I have to move, and I need a new family and a new religion and a new house. I need to start all over; everything is terrible. But what I usually need is, like, a glass of water." I did the same thing with spending money: "My boss is mad at me. I'll show him and spend my paycheck at my favorite store on a bunch of clothes I'd never wear," "My boyfriend dumped me, ha-ha, I'll take a trip I can't afford to get over it." I didn't know what I wanted out of life, so I'd buy a new phone or pair of shoes.

THE TRUE COST OF FAST FASHION

When considering a new, more eco-friendly wardrobe, the expense and options can be overwhelming. Instead of replacing your entire wardrobe, think about your transition as a piece-by-piece mission. The most eco-friendly thing you can do is to consume less by using what you have. Use it all the way up, and when it's time to replace it, consider the following questions recommended by our eco-fashion expert, Shannon Lohr:

1. Where was it made?
2. How was it made?
3. What is it made of?
4. Is it timeless and made to last, so I'll wear it for years to come?
5. Do I already have something similar in my closet?

And consider your needs, too. Ask the following questions so you can be satisfied with fewer purchases:

Does it fit?

Does it feel good?

Do I enjoy wearing it?

Is it versatile?

In addition to Factory45, Shannon created Market45 (https://market45.co) a one-stop shop for ethical and sustainable fashion. In terms of expense, eco-friendly fashion is becoming more and more accessible, but it's unlikely that prices will compare with some of your fast-fashion go-tos. Just remember that there is always a price to pay. It may not be in the dollars you spend, but someone is paying. For more insight on that, watch the documentary *The True Cost*.

This may sound naive, but it never occurred to me that when I was picking out a standard white button-down shirt from my favorite department store, someone across the world was working in substandard conditions sewing on those buttons, bleaching the fabric, and otherwise actually making the shirt. I thought it all came from a machine.

Similarly, before becoming a vegetarian and turning my attention to how food ended up on my plate, I didn't consider the food production practices that were affecting animals, other people, and the planet. It was too hard to think about. And even when I did start thinking about it, it wasn't an overnight transformation. Instead, I gave up eating cows for a while, then pigs, then chickens, and so on. All the while, I researched the changes I was making and found ways to build in inspiration and motivation to continue. I'm doing the same thing right now with my wardrobe and cosmetics.

Change isn't always easy, and it can be challenging to make new habits stick, but if you're willing to change slowly and thoughtfully, it's easier than you think. Be patient and curious as you look into how you want to shift things in your closet and your life. Ask questions of yourself and of people who have made the changes themselves.

Remember, too, that the tiny steps matter. For instance, just by reading an article a day for thirty days about something you're curious about, you can shift your mind-set and the way you think about things, which makes it easier to make the bigger changes. And again, nothing has to happen overnight. This is the main reason I don't recommend getting rid of your extra things when trying Project 333. Instead, create conditions to experience what it's like to dress with less without actually owning less. It's also why I'm not throwing out all my clothes and replacing them with eco-friendly pieces all at once, because that move in itself will have a bigger footprint: I'm consuming more and sending more waste into the world. Even if I donated everything, chances are that it will end up in a landfill sooner or later.

Speaking of landfills, someone once asked me how to let go of their things to live a life with less stuff and more freedom. She said, "I don't want to contribute to more stuff in landfills." I said, "You made that contribution from the moment you purchased the item." We all do. One day, it will all be in a landfill unless we come up with more creative ways to reuse and dispose of our things. That shouldn't prevent us from letting go of the excess we own, but it should inspire us to break the "consume, donate, consume, donate" cycle.

RECYCLING AND UPCYCLING

As mentioned earlier in Shannon's shocking Sustainable Fashion Facts, 95 percent of all clothing can be recycled or upcycled. Sometimes it feels easier to throw something away, but if you're willing to be creative, you may think of other ways to dispose of

your clothes. Here are a few ideas:

- Misti Nolen (@recycledyarn on Instagram) turns old sweaters back into yarn.
- The Renewal Workshop (https://renewalworkshop.com) takes discarded apparel and outerwear and turns it into "renewed apparel."
- Project Repat (http://projectrepat.com) keeps T-shirts out of landfills by turning them into memorable quilts.
- Factory45'er Regenerous Designs (http://regenerousdesigns.com) makes accessories and jewelry out of discarded designer fabric that would otherwise go into a landfill.
- Zero Waste Daniel (http://zerowastedaniel.com) makes designer clothing out of discarded fabric scraps.
- Recover (http://www.recovertex.com) turns textile waste into new yarn.

You'll find more resources for recycling and upcycling on the Project 333 Resources page, https://bemorewithless.com /project333-resources.

BUT STILL, LET GO

Don't hold on to stuff you don't wear because you're afraid of contributing waste. I know you want your stuff to go to the perfect place, but instead of holding on, waiting for perfection, repurpose it or give it to the best possible place and move on. The good you will be able to do in the world after letting go will be far more powerful than spending extra time holding on to something you don't want or need anymore. Check out local options for donations and find an extensive list of where to donate your stuff here: https://bemorewithless.com/project333 -resources. I think it's fair to say that if you're reading this book, you're curious about how to improve your life and the world on some level. That intention, fueled with moving through the world in a lighter way, will ensure you take better care of the earth and better care of you, inspiring others to do the same.

To learn more about slow fashion and better, more eco-friendly options (especially if you don't have time to research), follow our Project 333 eco expert, Shannon Lohr, on Instagram @factory45co. You can find Shannon's Project 333 wardrobe list on the Project 333 Resources page (https://bemorewithless.com /project333-resources) or subscribe to her newsletter at https:// factory45.co. You'll love her eco wisdom.

DECISIONS

ADULTS MAKE AN AVERAGE OF 35,000 DECISIONS A day. No wonder we're tired. Between food, money, family, health, work, and, yes, wardrobe decisions, we're inundated with choices and options. Choice should be a good thing, but once we have too many choices, there is diminishing return. We are fortunate to have the freedom to choose, but according to Barry Schwartz, author of *The Paradox of Choice: Why More Is Less*, we aren't happier because of it. Schwartz says, "When people have no choice, life is almost unbearable. As the number of available choices increases, as it has in our consumer culture, the autonomy, control, and liberation this variety brings are powerful and positive. But as the number of choices keeps growing, negative aspects of having a multitude of options begin to appear. As the number of choices grows further, the negatives escalate until we become overloaded. At this point, choice no longer liberates, but debilitates."

Have you ever experienced debilitating decision fatigue? I think it's in those most debilitating moments that we give up and turn on mindless TV so we don't have to choose anymore. Or we tune out in other ways, and while that's still a choice, it's a choice to stop feeling, to stop choosing, if only for a few minutes or hours. Decision fatigue is real. We may not get so fatigued that we can't make more decisions, but the quality of our decision-making suffers as we move throughout the day. It may seem like most of the decisions we make come from external sources like demands from work, email, and other obligations, but we put a lot of the decision fatigue burden on ourselves. Lack of planning, and loading up our lives with excess clutter, commitments, choices, and chaos, increases decision fatigue and simply wears us out.

By streamlining some of the decisions we have to make over and over again, we can create more clarity for decisions that may matter more, and build our resilience against decision fatigue when situations arise that demand more from us. For instance, instead of deciding what to eat several times a day, choose to eat similar meals throughout the week. Check email and other social media less frequently. And if you've ever tried on more than one outfit getting ready for the day, or felt stressed about what to wear for a meeting or event, chances are your closet is adding to decision fatigue because there are too many choices in there. While Project 333 will eliminate any closet-generated decision fatigue, there are other ways to do it, too. Create a decision-free wardrobe with Project 333 or by implementing one or more of these decision-free (or decision-lite) recommendations:

1. CREATE A UNIFORM. There's a reason world leaders, CEOs, entrepreneurs, and others dress in a self-imposed uniform. It removes the question "What should I wear?" If you're raising a family and making decisions for your children, or building a business, or serving a community, do you really want to spend time on trivial concerns about what to wear? Matilda Kahl, an art director in New York City, explained why she wears the same thing to work every day in an article she wrote for *Harper's Bazaar*: "The simple choice of wearing a work uniform has saved me countless wasted hours thinking, 'What the hell am I going to wear today?' And in fact, these black trousers and white blouses have become an important daily reminder that frankly, I'm in control." She also added, "To state the obvious, a work uniform is not an original idea. There's a group of people that have embraced this way of dressing for years—they call it a *suit*."

2. ONLY INCLUDE SEASONALLY APPROPRIATE CLOTHES. There's no need to sort through your sweaters to get to your sundresses in summer, or to search for your winter boots in a pile of sandals. Get the stuff you aren't wearing out of sight so you don't even have to think about it until you're actually going to wear it.

3. DRESS MONOCHROMATICALLY. Don't worry about the pressure to dress with lots of different colors and patterns. Instead, dress in all black, blue, white, or your favorite color to wear.

4. SHIFT YOUR FOCUS. Notice your thoughts around what you wear. Shift your focus when you think any of the following:

   - I HAVE NOTHING TO WEAR.
   - I'M BORED WITH MY WARDROBE.
   - I DESERVE SOMETHING NEW.
   - EVERYONE WILL NOTICE I'M WEARING THIS AGAIN.

   Instead, remind yourself that you have enough and that you have more important things to focus on. Remember that shopping for new clothes won't cure boredom (curiosity does that), that you deserve way more than something new to wear, *and* that no one cares what you're wearing.

5. SHOP LESS. If choosing from hundreds of items in your closet isn't exhausting enough, what about when we walk into a store and have thousands of items to choose from, or millions on the internet? Search for a new shirt on Amazon and you'll have 300,000 choices, or dial it in and Google "black dress." There are 291,000,000 options for "black dress" at the time of this book's writing. Now of course, you'd narrow your search results, but that involves decision-making, too. Project 333 invites you to

shop every three months, or even less often, depending on what you really need to shift into a new season.

WHY DO WE SPEND SO MUCH ENERGY GETTING DRESSED, SHOPPING, AND DECIDING WHAT TO WEAR?

1. WE ARE UNSATISFIED OR INSECURE. Marketers remind us constantly that we aren't good enough, and that if we owned and wore the right things, we would be happy and content. We are exposed to more than five thousand advertising messages a day, compared to five hundred in the 1970s (which still sounds like too many). As an ex–advertising executive, I can tell you that it is the job of the ad agencies, magazines, billboards, and other marketing messages to convince you that you will be a better person, more beautiful, successful, and loved, if you buy only what they are offering. And until we say "enough is enough," they will continue to succeed.

2. WE CARE WAY TOO MUCH ABOUT WHAT OTHER PEOPLE THINK OF US. All the effort I put into demonstrating who I was by what I wore went unnoticed. When I started the challenge, I was working full-time in advertising sales for magazines targeting a very affluent audience. No one noticed I was wearing the

same few things for three months. My colleagues didn't notice, my clients didn't notice—no one noticed or cared.

By choosing what to wear from a small capsule wardrobe, you'll get to wear your favorite things every day and eliminate decision fatigue. Save your brainpower for more meaningful decisions, creative ideas, and problem-solving throughout the day. When we create boundaries around things that are distracting us from what really matters, our level of engagement in the things we actually care about becomes boundless.

CRAZY

WOULDN'T IT BE CRAZY IF . . . ? THIS ONE QUESTION HAS led me down a path of remarkable changes and adventure in my life. Whenever I think, *Wouldn't it be crazy if . . .* , I can't help but smile. This question used to scare me so much that I'd shut it down immediately. I'd start to think, *Wouldn't it be crazy if . . .* , quickly followed by, *Stop, that's crazy, be reasonable. Be practical.* Now that I've explored several of my crazy ideas and seen the wonderful things that can happen when I see them through, whenever those words come into my head, I'm immediately intrigued by the possibilities of my "crazy" idea. Before I got sick and answered my wake-up call, and before I simplified my life by paying off debt and getting rid of clutter, I dismissed most of my crazy ideas. I stuck with the plan instead. Work hard, climb the ladder, keep people-pleasing and make ends meet (all with a big smile on your face)—aka ignore what you really need and burn out trying to do it all the "right way."

Once I created more time and space in my life through simplicity, I decided to consider the question "Wouldn't it be crazy if . . ." more often because I didn't want things to be normal or the same anymore. The right way wasn't working for our family. Normal didn't make me happy or healthy. And as I questioned the definition of "normal," I thought about how I strived to be the normal version of successful, all while letting other people define what *successful* meant.

Here are a few examples of some of the "crazy" ideas I've actually followed through on that—in the end— yielded very nice results:

WOULDN'T IT BE CRAZY IF WE SELL OUR HOUSE? We did it and downsized to an apartment less than half the size, with no storage space. Now our free time is really free.

WOULDN'T IT BE CRAZY IF I QUIT MY JOB? With a solid exit strategy that took sixteen months to execute, I gave my notice and walked away from an almost twenty-year career. Scary? YES! Worth it? So much more YES!

WOULDN'T IT BE CRAZY TO DRESS WITH 33 ITEMS OR LESS FOR 3 MONTHS? I started Project 333 in 2010. I can't imagine how much money and time I've saved with this crazy idea, and now you're reading a book about it.

WOULDN'T IT BE CRAZY IF I TOOK MY TINY WARDROBE ON TOUR? In January 2015, I committed to visiting thirty-three cities with my tiny wardrobe. I've been to thirty-five-plus, and will be vising many more. I've met the best like-hearted people, explored new cities, and shared how dressing with less and simplifying my life has changed me in the best ways.

Those are only a few of my crazy ideas, and I know there are many more to come. Usually when I think, *Wouldn't it be crazy if . . .* , my default answer is, *I could never do that.* As soon as the word *never* crosses my mind, I know I'm on to something. Whenever I think, *I could never* or *That's crazy*, I know I need more information and that I've identified a new area in which to grow and change.

The typical stages of considering Project 333 include:

- THAT'S CRAZY.
- HMMM, I'M CURIOUS.
- OMG, WHY DID I WAIT SO LONG
  TO GET STARTED? THIS IS AWESOME!

How long each stage lasts is different for everyone.

WE LIKE TO DISMISS THINGS WE AREN'T SURE ABOUT BY LABELING THEM

A *Vogue* marketing director called Project 333 "severe" and said it wasn't for "most people." Some may have dismissed the challenge as crazy or impossible as a result. Tens of thousands of people from around the world have discovered otherwise. Call it weird or crazy, but not severe. Dressing with less isn't a sacrifice, and surprisingly, the "challenge" isn't that challenging for most people.

Here are a few things that are severe or extreme. Things that deserve our attention. Things that aren't changing our lives in a positive way.

WHAT'S SEVERE IS . . .

We spend money we don't have on clothes we don't wear. When I was deep in debt, the saying "Walk a mile in someone else's shoes" took on a whole new meaning for me. I didn't actually own my shoes or most of the items in my closet. Instead, I was paying the minimum amount on my credit cards, which didn't begin to cover the cost of my actual wardrobe. And the icing on the cake was that there I was, living paycheck to paycheck, charging my way into a smile with a new pair of jeans or the (not so) perfect little black dress, even while there were clothes in my closet with tags still attached. I wasn't even wearing the clothes I couldn't afford. This is severe.

We assess our value with the size of our waist. How many days have you let the scale, or the way your pants fit, dictate your mood for the day? It seems the tides are changing here, but I grew up trying every diet out there, always trying to be smaller, but mostly just feeling bad about myself when I got on the scale or tried on clothes, or when items I already owned didn't fit well. My size says nothing about me. This is severe.

We follow rules for getting dressed. Why do we have to dress for our body type, skin tone, or age? And why are we always dressing to look skinnier or looking for items that make us appear smaller? In *Beyond Beautiful: A Practical Guide to Being Happy, Confident, and You in a Looks-Obsessed World*, author Anuschka Rees says, "The idea that our clothes should be 'appropriate' for our body type, such a regular topic in magazines and our day-to-day conversations, reflects the scary extent to which we have all internalized that looking slim and attractive according to today's societal ideals is much more important than wearing clothes you personally like, self-expression, and having fun with fashion." Boom. That's severe.

I prefer wearing clothes I can live in, clothes that fit my body as it is and not as it "should be." The ad execs creating the ads and the marketers convincing you to buy aren't wearing what they're selling, either. Really, they aren't. Because they aren't selling clothes. They are selling a feeling or a lifestyle. They know that elusive thing they're trying to convince you that you're missing is manufactured and made up. Their focus is making sure you feel less than enough so they can offer you something to buy. This is severe. Labeling Project 333 and other challenges, lifestyles, or things you may not understand at first as "severe," "extreme," or "impossible" discounts your curiosity, resolve, and desire for change. This minimalist fashion challenge isn't severe. It's an experiment, and with the right approach, you'll have a little fun and open doors you never knew existed.

WHY YOU SHOULD ALWAYS CHALLENGE YOUR "NEVERS"

There are occasional "never" statements that are sound and logical, especially when they protect you from destructive behavior. Aside from that, most "never" statements are simply self-limiting beliefs. Whenever you say "never"—and it's probably more often than you think—pay attention to the statement. "Never" robs us of better health, work, love, and happiness. "Never" keeps us comfortable and complacent. If your "never" is too scary to consider at first, write it down and come back to it.

Here are a few examples of "never" statements I've said and heard from others:

- I COULD NEVER BE DEBT-FREE.
- I COULD NEVER QUIT MY JOB.
- I WILL NEVER GIVE UP MEAT/SUGAR/ BREAD/[INSERT FAVORITE FOOD].
- I COULD NEVER START MY OWN BUSINESS.
- I WILL NEVER LEAVE THIS TOWN.
- I COULD NEVER GIVE UP

  _____.

- I WILL NEVER TRY _____.
- I WILL NEVER CHANGE

  _____.

If self-imposed nevers aren't bad enough, we also assume nevers for everyone around us. "They will never support my decision." "He will never change." "She will never say yes." "They will never think I'm cool/talented/good enough." "Never" statements go on and on, but they generally fall into three categories:

1. What you think you could never do or accomplish
2. What you think you would never give up or change
3. What you think others could never do, accomplish, give up, or change

What if "never" statements are really part of our bucket lists? What if nevers are what we want most, but because we don't want to be hurt, or fail, or expose ourselves to disappointment, we keep them in the never file? We deserve to challenge our nevers. We should, at the very least, experience a taste of our nevers so we can make a fact-based decision on whether it should be left behind or become something that changes our lives and informs our work. Challenge your nevers. Everything will be okay. Better, even. When we make decisions based on facts instead of fear, we can change anything we want.

CURIOUS

THE FIRST REACTION TO PROJECT 333 ISN'T ALWAYS curiosity or interest. In fact, it's often denial or dismissal. If that's you, don't worry. Take a breath. Curiosity will follow. I think this is often our first reaction to something that doesn't fit into our normal day-to-day way of thinking. I'm guilty of it myself, and I am sure that if I hadn't created Project 333, I'd dismiss it, too (at first). Our ego quietly reminds us that change is scary. It says, "I don't want to change." And then at some point, our heart reminds us, "Oh yes, I do want something to change. Maybe this is the first step."

Now that there are ten years of research and experimenting behind this crazy closet challenge, you can be curious not just about how you will change your wardrobe but how you can change parts of your life, or your whole life, through it. While I noticed benefits like easier mornings, saving money, and less stress, I never imagined that people would be reducing depression and anxiety, changing careers, simplifying their entire homes, or starting new businesses because they tried Project 333. I learn more and more about myself and others on almost a daily basis. I'm not exaggerating when I say I receive emails and messages on social media (Facebook, Twitter, Instagram) about Project 333 daily. Search #project333 on Instagram, and you'll see what I'm talking about.

If you feel like you might be in the dismissal phase while considering Project 333, stay open. Keep reading, ask questions, and imagine your closet with a fraction of the items that currently reside there. Elizabeth Gilbert says, "I think curiosity is our friend that teaches us how to become ourselves."

In the next chapter, I'll share some questions to ask yourself, but don't feel limited to those questions. Be curious and explore as you consider the challenge before starting it and then all the way through it. Notice what's happening. So often we forget to notice or we get too busy to notice, or we think we're too busy to notice, but isn't that what being alive is all about? Noticing our lives? We are born noticing, and then we're taught that we're supposed to do things a certain way, and over time, in an effort to fit ourselves into the right mold, we stop noticing. We stop noticing what makes us smile, what makes us sad, what makes us feel good, feel bad, feel interested, feel tired. And we say it's because we're too busy or because we're too consumed with taking care of everything and everyone around us, but one thing I've noticed about noticing is that when you forget about yourself, you probably aren't noticing what's best serving the life around you, either. If the only thing this challenge does is help you begin to notice things about you, it will be worth it.

THE VALUE OF CHALLENGES AND
PERSONAL EXPERIMENTS

How will you know the truth if you believe everything you think? Things changed dramatically when I stopped believing everything I thought. Instead of listening to the fear inside that told me I couldn't do something and encouraged me to stay safe and comfortable, I chose to experiment and learn what was really true and what was best for me. I experiment a lot.

> I lived with only 100 items for a few months.
>
> I dress with 33 items or less every three months.
>
> I traveled for a month with only a carry-on bag.
>
> I follow the Whole30 food program for 30 days several times a year, abstaining from sugar, grains, dairy, alcohol, and processed food.

The value of these personal experiments and challenges is that they've given me the opportunity to experience the truth instead of assuming it. Project 333 is a great example of a personal challenge, but there are many others. You can create your own, too.

Try one of these experiments/challenges (especially if you think you could never do it):

ONLY PACK FOR HALF THE DAYS YOU ARE TRAVELING. Have you ever noticed that you bring every possible thing you can fit into your bags when traveling? And that you rarely need it all, but you keep bringing it, trip after trip, just in case? Try half. If you're traveling for two days, pack for one. (More on this in the travel chapter.)

ONLY POST POSITIVE COMMENTS AND IDEAS ON SOCIAL MEDIA FOR A MONTH. The easiest way to vent our negativity is to post it on the socials. Commit to only positivity when posting to Facebook, Twitter, or other social media. This might make you more aware of other negativity. If it's not adding value to your social feeds or life, unfollow or unsubscribe. Remember, we get what we accept. I don't accept other people's negativity into my life, unless it motivates me to do better or be better, or to help them do better or be better (usually that's not the case).

TRY A WHOLE30. Eat real food and eliminate the following from your diet for 30 days: sugar, dairy, processed foods, grains, legumes, alcohol. No weighing yourself, either. Just like Project 333 isn't about the clothes, Whole30 isn't about the scale. For more information, see https://whole30.com.

GIVE UP FACEBOOK FOR 90 DAYS. If you think Facebook or other social channels may be draining you instead of fueling you, give them up. Remove the apps from your phone, suspend your accounts, and get on with your life. You won't miss a thing.

THE MINIMALISM GAME. Enjoy this decluttering challenge from Joshua and Ryan at theminimalists.com: Find a friend or family member, someone who's willing to get rid of their excess stuff. Each of you must get rid of one thing on the first day. On the second, two things. Three items on the third. And so on and so forth. Anything can go! Clothes, furniture, electronics, tools, decorations, etc. Donate, sell, or recycle/trash. Whatever you do, each material possession must be out of your house—and out of your life—by midnight each day.

GIVE AWAY ONE THING A DAY FOR A WHOLE YEAR. Simple enough, but at the end of the year, you'll be 365 items lighter.

WRITE LOTS OF THANK-YOU NOTES. Commit to one hundred, or one per week, or write one thank-you note every day for a year like Gina Hamadey (@thankyouyear on Instagram). We always have something to be grateful for.

ONLY CHECK EMAIL ONCE A DAY, OR ONCE A WEEK. If you want to get out of your inbox and into your life, schedule daily checks instead of leaving your email open or responding to notifications. The internet is open 24/7, but you don't have to be.

THE BUSY BOYCOTT. If you want to trade your busy life for a full one, try this 21-day challenge: https://bemorewithless.com/the-busy-boycott-challenge.

PROJECT 333. I recommend starting here.

HOW TO CREATE YOUR OWN EXPERIMENTS

If you're curious about something, or struggling to make a change, make it fun. Create your own experiment. All you have to do is identify the problem or subject matter. Make a list of questions, then create a challenge with time constraints and rules. Share with friends and family or on social media with your own hashtag for extra accountability. Your potential for growth is directly proportional to what you're willing to consider. Be curious.

QUESTIONS

ONE OF THE MOST IMPORTANT THINGS YOU CAN DO before beginning this wardrobe challenge, or taking on any big change, is to identify why you want to do it. Why is always more important (and interesting) than how. It's easy to figure out the how. You can ask people or read books or articles. Google always knows how, too. Your why (or whys, plural) will give any change you make its sticking power. Use your why as leverage when things get tough or when you lose motivation to continue. Your why for starting Project 333 might be because you think it will be fun, or because you want to pay off debt, or because you're sick and tired of never having anything to wear (even though your closet is stuffed with clothes). Or maybe, like me, you just want a little peace. There is no right or wrong answer, and don't be surprised if your answers change over time.

Take some inspiration from the previous chapter on curiosity and answer the following questions before, during, and after your Project 333 challenge. If you feel like skipping this chapter, it's probably because you've never questioned your consumption habits or feelings about your clothing. It might not seem important, but taking the time to answer these questions will have a big impact on how successful you are with the challenge. Your answers may surprise you. Remember, change attempted slowly and thoughtfully lasts. Take the time to be insightful during your challenge and give it a chance to effect real change in your life. You deserve that. Grab a pen and a piece of paper or a journal and get writing. Make a cup of tea, or turn on some gentle music if that helps you settle in and open up. Don't edit or judge your answers. You don't have to share them with anyone or even reread them, although you may want to.

QUESTIONS TO ASK BEFORE YOU GET STARTED

Answering these questions will give you some conviction and motivation to move forward. If your answer is "I don't know," come back later and ask again. You may know more than you're willing to admit at first.

Why do you want to try Project 333?

What was your first reaction to hearing about Project 333?

Is that how you react to other new ideas that are unconventional?

What are some of the things you've heard about it that make you interested?

Are there specific things you want to learn about or challenge yourself on within the challenge?

What are your biggest fears or concerns about making this three-month commitment?

How will you stay accountable?

Is there anyone you want to invite to join in?

ASK THE FOLLOWING QUESTIONS WHEN EVALUATING YOUR CURRENT WARDROBE AND THINKING ABOUT WHAT ITEMS TO INCLUDE. Answering these questions will reveal some really interesting things about yourself in terms of how you use your clothing. When you finish the challenge, revisit these questions. Don't be surprised if your answers are completely different. You'll be different, too.

What are your three favorite outfits?

Which pieces do you wear most frequently (even though you have many other choices)? Describe each piece.

What colors do you most enjoy wearing?

What colors are hanging in your closet?

What pieces in your closet would you never wear? Why are they still in your closet?

Is any of the clothing in your closet uncomfortable to wear (too small, too big, scratchy material)? Why is that clothing still in your closet? ***If you've just had a lightbulb moment, feel free to pause and remove all the uncomfortable, unwearable clothes from your closet. You deserve to wear clothes that feel good on your body!***

Describe your lifestyle: Do you work outside the home? Are you active? Do you entertain frequently?

Do you tend to wear out your clothes quickly?

Do you create a different version of yourself through your clothing for different activities or for different people?

Are you an aspirational shopper (buying things for a life you wish you had)?

Do you love a good sale?

Do you love telling everyone about the great deal you got?

Did you get the clothes you wear most on sale or while impulse shopping?

Are there pieces in your closet that you got for 50 percent off that still have their tags?

Who are the people who encourage you to shop? Are there other ways you can spend time with them while you're doing this challenge?

Is shopping your favorite sport?

What makes you want to shop, or when do you typically crave something new?

How long does the high of a new purchase last?

If you could start over and buy all new clothing, what items would you include on your list?

If your closet were a store and you had to shop there, what would you buy again? What would you leave hanging?

Estimate how much money you have spent on clothing, jewelry, accessories, and shoes over the past ten years (gulp). If you had that sum of money in your hands right now, would you spend it on the same items? Other clothes? Something else completely?

What would it feel like to put away all your jewelry and accessories, except for your favorite scarf and necklace, for three months?

DURING PROJECT 333

Answer these questions once you start the challenge. These questions are less about your clothes and more about you, but then again, so is Project 333.

Who do you love?

What do you care about?

What/who makes you laugh so hard you cry?

What's that one thing you've been wanting to try but have never gotten around to?

How do you take care of yourself?

If you had more time each day, how would you spend it? Each week? Each year?

If you had less stress and more calm in your life, how would you feel?

What causes are you passionate about?

What do you do out of obligation instead of genuine interest?

What are three things you said yes to recently when you wanted to say no?

If you invested the time, money, and energy that you used on shopping, sales, and building your wardrobe in something that really mattered, what would you create?

Can you admit that you have enough?

Can you rejoice in the fact that you *are* enough?

BEFORE YOU START ANOTHER SEASON OF PROJECT 333

Ask these questions toward or at the end of your first three months of dressing with less.

What did you love about the challenge?

What did you hate about the challenge?

Would you recommend the challenge to friends? Why?

What surprised you about Project 333?

Was it harder or easier than you thought it would be?

If you could remove one rule or add one rule, what would it be?

How could you shift the challenge rules to work even better in your life?

Some of these questions will be hard, and maybe you don't know the answers. Revisit some of the earlier questions you may have struggled with each month during your first season of Project 333. Again, don't edit or judge or be surprised if this work leads you in a completely different direction than what you expect.

CLEAN

BEFORE YOU START THE CHALLENGE AND CHOOSE your 33-item wardrobe, do a full-on closet clean-out to motivate and inspire your three-month challenge. There is something about a clean slate that screams, "Let's get started!"

Closet purging and decluttering can be a lifelong battle. Until I started dressing with 33 items or less every 3 months, I cleaned out my closet seasonally. I'd go through my clothes every few months, move things around, take a little out, and add more in. I'd drag storage containers in from the garage, swap out seasonal items, donate a few things, try to make a little space, and then go shopping to celebrate a new season. Notice the vicious cycle I had going here? Until Project 333, my solutions were only temporary. I always had a deep desire to fill all the spaces I had cleaned out. It wasn't just my closet, either. I did the same thing while decluttering my home. It was never permanent. If you want room to breathe, to create, to pause, to dream, to spend time with people you love, or to know who you are and what matters to you, stop filling all the spaces. As we declutter and let go of stuff, busyness, overthinking, and heartache, things may feel empty at first. And empty can hurt. So we fill the spaces to relieve the pain. Then we start all over again.

STOP FILLING ALL THE SPACES

When you move into a new home, or if you've recently decluttered your home, don't rush out and buy everything each room is "supposed" to have. Live in the space and then decide what you want or need. It's up to you, and it's much less than anyone would have you believe. Stop filling all the spaces in your home with the right stuff.

After a breakup or breakdown, be willing to feel the emptiness and wait for the lessons. Stop filling all the spaces with busyness, shopping, food, booze, or other numbing devices. They won't prevent the pain, only delay it.

When you declutter your closet, empty hangers are not a shopping invitation. Dress with less and decide what "enough" means to you. Stop filling all the spaces with clothing that doesn't fit your body or your lifestyle.

If you find yourself waiting in line or sitting in traffic, or are simply settling down after a long day, take a few deep breaths and reflect. Stop filling all the spaces with digital distractions and mindless scrolling. Just let there be space.

When an appointment cancels or something falls off your to-do list, don't replace it. Embrace the margin. Stop filling all the spaces with more to-do items. Less do. More be.

Resist. Wait. Breathe. Instead, let the extra spaces in your home and on your calendar and in your mind or heart be empty for a while. The emptiness may be uncomfortable at first, but that's where the answers lie. And when it's time, you'll have room for what you really want.

THE ULTIMATE CLOSET CLEANOUT

Have fun with this step-by-step guide to cleaning out your closet. This could be the last time you ever have to do it.

PREP

Schedule your ultimate closet cleanout. Put it on your calendar. Depending on the state of your closet, you may need two to five hours, or even more. Clear the day, hire a sitter, unplug, and make it important.

Make two playlists: one with your favorite happy, uplifting, "everything is going to be okay" music, and one filled with songs that calm you down. You're going to need good music.

Fill a water bottle. This is a marathon. You will need water (and snacks).

LET'S GO!

Empty your closet. Yes, the whole thing. Completely empty. Don't worry about sorting yet—just move everything onto your bed. If you put everything on your bed, you'll be motivated to complete the project before bedtime.

If you have clothes in bureaus, storage containers, or other areas of your home, get those, too. Dump them on the bed. While you're at it, add your shoes, accessories, and jewelry. All the things.

Wash your closet. Make it really clean in there. Air it out.

Take a break. This is a great time to take a walk. Get away from your closet, clothes, and guilt, frustration, or any other emotions that are coming up. Walk and breathe. Let go.

LET'S GO AGAIN!

Drink some water and turn up the music.

Move the clothes on your bed into three piles on the floor in a ruthless first-pass sort. Don't give it too much thought—just go with your first reaction. Sort items into the following piles:

> LOVE: "I love these items. They fit me well, and I wear them frequently."

> MAYBE: "I want to keep this, but I don't know why" (you know you have those items).

> TOSS: "These items don't fit my body or my life," or "These items are in poor condition" (repurpose if possible). Your toss pile will include items for donations and the dump.

Keep going until your bed is clear and you have three piles on the floor.

Roll around on your bed, kick your feet up in the air, and scream, "Almost there!"

Take another break. Drink some water and eat some snacks.

LAST PASS!

Box or bag up your items to donate and bring them to your car or garage. Get them out of sight immediately.

Throw out anything you've deemed trash.

Take a last pass at your two remaining piles. Try on clothing you aren't sure about, and ask the following questions:

"Would I go to the store and buy this today?"

"Will I wear this in the next three to six months— or ever?" If the answer is no, start a new toss pile, then immediately add those items to your donation box. Out of sight.

Put the remaining items back in your closet or into storage containers if you won't be wearing them this season.

Even though Project 333 officially lasts for only three months, consider this closet cleanout the beginning of a permanent change, the beginning of finding comfort even in the empty spaces, the beginning of finding better ways to soothe your pain. Yes, you may have to clean things up again, but plan to have less to let go of next time. Say good-bye to spring cleaning, stressful seasonal wardrobe rotations, and the thought of lugging around hundreds of heavy hangers the next time you move.

ELIMINATE

THE PROCESS OF ELIMINATING ITEMS FROM YOUR wardrobe can be daunting. Letting go and decluttering is a major part of simplifying your closet and life, but ironically, this part of simplicity can be complicated and overwhelming. What should you keep, donate, or sell? How do you sell? Where do you donate? Make it easier for yourself by eliminating the obvious suspects, like the things that don't fit you (and haven't fit for years), and the things you've never worn.

If you're having trouble coming up with anything to eliminate, start with this list of 33 things:

1. Anything with shoulder pads, even if they're making a comeback.
2. Your high school jeans that haven't buttoned since high school.

3. That formal outfit or bridesmaid dress you bought for one occasion (even though you said you could wear it again).

4. Your ex-anyone's anything.

5. Christmas sweaters (please).

6. Things that are ripped or have holes that aren't supposed to be there.

7. See-through things.

8. Those super-cute shoes you can't walk in.

9. Sentimental items that make you sad.

10. The warm coat you don't wear. Someone needs it more than you.

11. Sentimental items that don't fit. Take a picture.

12. Clothes you're saving for your children (your kids don't want your stuff).

13. Things that need to go to the tailor that never go to the tailor.

14. Dry-clean-only items you've washed yourself and ruined.

15. Hats you don't wear, even though you think you might someday.

16. Ill-fitting bras. Feature your features.

17. Extra purses. You need only one (I know, the truth hurts).

18. Clothes that don't belong to you. Give them back.

19. Anything with a weird smell that won't wash out.

20. Anything that leaves a mark or blister anywhere on your body.
21. Scarves that don't go with anything you currently own.
22. Clothes that don't allow your underwear to be under.
23. Anything you have to squeeze into or can't breathe in. Breathing is good.
24. Clothes you bought on vacation that you won't wear where you live.
25. Pants that are shorter than they are supposed to be.
26. Shirts that are longer than they are supposed to be.
27. Sequins and sparkles, if you prefer simple and subtle.
28. Anything with a stain that won't come out.
29. Guilt items. If you spent too much for it, dump the guilt. You'll keep paying for it in time and attention if you don't let it go now.
30. Multiples. Just because the blazer looked good in navy doesn't mean you need it in every color. One is enough.
31. The unmatched top or bottom of a suit. They aren't sold separately for a reason.
32. Clothes you can pet.
33. Yoga pants that don't go to yoga.

Most of these items have made an appearance in my closet (even sequins), and I don't miss any of them. If you had a strong reaction to anything on the list or have every item in your closet, take a deep breath. This list is slightly tongue-in-cheek, and, of course, you have to decide what to keep and what to donate, but ask yourself why you're holding on to things you don't wear. Getting rid of clutter and learning to let go can be challenging, so simplify the process by creating guidelines for yourself so you know what to donate, sell, or save. Here are some of the guidelines I used and recommend. That doesn't mean they'll be an exact fit for you—use them or tweak them a bit so you don't have to make new decisions for each item.

SELL IF:

You are in debt and the item is worth $50 or more. When it comes to clothing and accessories, it's hard to get your money back by reselling. You can sell through a local or online consignment store, but it may be more trouble than it's worth. Really think about how valuable your time is. Are you willing to spend hours of time and energy to sell the clothes you don't wear anymore? If you're in debt and will be using your earnings to pay down debt, it may make sense. I recommend donating your lower-priced items and trying to sell some of your higher-end brand-name handbags or jewelry. You may have better luck grouping items and selling lots of clothing; for instance, sell five dresses together instead of separately. I didn't sell any of my wardrobe, but we did sell other items in our home to help pay down debt.

You aren't in debt but have extra time on your hands and want to spend that time selling stuff.

DO NOT SELL IF:

You are short on time, don't want to be bothered, or have better things to do.

DONATE IF:

You want to make space more quickly. The quickest way to get rid of your stuff is to donate it. Box it up and get it out of sight, then either drive it to a local donation center or see more recommendations here: https://bemorewithless.com/project333-resources.

You are out of debt and you'd rather protect your time than chase more money.

An organization you're passionate about supporting actually needs donations.

Donate to good places, but don't worry about finding the perfect place for each thing. When our family was downsizing from our 2,000-square-foot home to a small apartment, there were some items we didn't know what to do with. Instead of holding on to them and delaying our progress, we dragged it all onto our driveway. We photographed the pile of stuff and placed a local classified ad with the picture, our address, and the simple description "free stuff." Everything was gone within 15 minutes.

If you can't let go because you're worried you'll miss the stuff or have to buy it again, prove yourself right or wrong by hiding it first. Box it up without labeling the boxes and get it out of sight for a few months. If you do miss it or need something in the boxes, bring it back into the house (not the whole box, just the thing you miss). If you can't remember it (which is most often the case) or don't miss it, let it go without fear.

DON'T DONATE IF:

You are in debt and can put a dent in your debt by selling your stuff.

SAVE IF:

You know you'll use it again. For instance, if you're in between jobs, considering more children, moving, or there is something else going on in your life where you know you'll be able to reuse things you aren't using right now, save it. And of course, save items you wear or use seasonally, like winter coats, skis, and bathing suits.

DON'T SAVE IF:

You think your kids want it. I often hear from parents that they can't let go of something because they're saving it for their children. Then I hear from adult children who don't know how to tell their parents they don't want their stuff. There is only one way to know if your adult children want your stuff (or their old stuff that you're storing for them): Ask them. I know this is a revolutionary idea, but try having a conversation. If they say yes, give it to them. Especially if they have their own homes. I can think of very few circumstances where parents should be holding on to their adult children's things or saving things of their own for their adult children. If, when asked, adult children say, "I don't want anything," believe them and let go. And by all means, don't take it personally. They love you, not your things.

You are holding on "just in case." The "just in case" excuse is a messy combination of fear and procrastination. We hold on because we aren't quite ready to let go, but we rarely use or enjoy the "just in case" stuff we keep. Take a look in the back of your closet, in the junk drawer, under the sink, or in boxes in the garage or attic, and it's clear that "just in case" means "never." When we say, "I'll keep this just in case," what we're really saying is . . .

"I'm not ready."

"I'm afraid I'll need this."

"I'm afraid to let go."

"I'm afraid I won't have enough."

Admitting that "just in case" means "never" allows us to stop procrastinating and invites us to let go and stop living in fear of not having enough. When we say good-bye to "just in case," we can start living and giving in more meaningful ways.

As you are eliminating things, remind yourself that you aren't making space for more stuff, you are making space for more life.

CHALLENGE

HERE IT IS! WHILE ALL OF THE OTHER CHAPTERS IN this book will help you make Project 333 a meaningful experience and answer some of your questions, this is indeed the chapter that provides everything you need to know to get started. Perhaps you flipped through the book to find this chapter before reading anything else. Understandable, but I encourage you to revisit the earlier chapters for more inspiration and understanding before you begin. The "why to" get started is just as important as (if not more than) the "how to" you'll find here.

PROJECT 333: THE RULES

WHEN: Every three months. Officially, a new season of Project 333 begins January 1, April 1, June 1, and October 1, but it's never too late to start, so please join in anytime!

WHAT: 33 items, including:

- CLOTHING
- ACCESSORIES
- JEWELRY
- SHOES (ONE PAIR COUNTS AS ONE ITEM)

WHAT NOT: These items are *not* counted among your
33 items:

- WEDDING RING *OR* ONE
  OTHER SENTIMENTAL
  PIECE OF JEWELRY THAT
  YOU NEVER TAKE OFF
- UNDERWEAR
- SLEEPWEAR
- IN-HOME LOUNGEWEAR
- WORKOUT CLOTHING (BUT YOUR WORKOUT CLOTHES
  HAVE TO WORK OUT)

HOW: Choose your 33 items, box up the remainder of
your wardrobe, seal it with tape, and put it out of sight.
Don't give it away—just hide it for now.

WHAT ELSE: Consider that you are creating a wardrobe
that you can live, work, and play in for three months.
This is not a project in suffering. If your clothes don't fit
or are in poor condition, replace them.

These rules have been published all over the internet, as
well as in books and magazines. Even though you may have
seen them before, trust me when I say the rules bear repeating.
Take another look.

HOW TO START PROJECT 333

Reading this book will help you get started and keep you going while you're doing the challenge. If you skipped ahead to this chapter (totally what I would have done, too), go back and start from the beginning while you're doing the challenge to reinforce and support your decision to dress with less for the next three months. If it feels too challenging, or you get bored or frustrated, come back and read a chapter that you think might help you. If there isn't one, email me: courtney@bemorewith less.com.

When you're ready, follow these steps (or start with the Ultimate Closet Cleanout in chapter nine):

1. Take all your clothing from your closet and drawers and hidden storage boxes, and dump everything in a pile in one central location. *All* your clothing from every season should be in this one pile. The bed is a great place to dump everything because you'll be more determined to complete this part before nightfall/bedtime. You can break up this process over two days, but don't drag it out much longer or you'll overthink your decisions.

2. Choose clothing to wear for the next two days. Imagine you're packing for a trip. Set those items aside, or put them back in your closet. Now you know you have something to wear for a couple of days even if nothing else makes it back in the closet.

3. Create three clothing piles:

- LOVE: A PILE FOR THE STUFF YOU *LOVE* AND CANNOT BEAR TO PART WITH.

- TOSS: A PILE FOR CLOTHING THAT DOESN'T FIT OR ISN'T COMFORTABLE OR DOESN'T LOOK GOOD ON YOU OR THAT YOU HAVEN'T WORN IN A LONG TIME. LATER YOU CAN DECIDE WHAT TO DONATE, WHAT TO REPURPOSE, AND WHAT TO TRASH.

- MAYBE: IF YOU AREN'T SURE, POP IT IN THE MAYBE PILE. DON'T BE SURPRISED IF THIS IS YOUR BIGGEST PILE OF ITEMS.

4. Take a break. Hydrate, turn up the music, and laugh (because if you don't laugh, you might want to cry). Look at all your clothing, and laugh about how you didn't think you had anything to wear or that you were thinking about hitting up a sale this weekend looking for more.

5. Get back to work by eliminating one of your three piles. Box up and discard/donate your Toss pile. Instead of deciding what to save, sell, or donate, consider boxing and hiding all of it so you can revisit it with more clarity in three months. See chapter ten for guidelines on when to donate and when to sell. I recommend giving things away in most cases. They weren't making money in your closet, and they probably won't now, either. Instead, get paid immediately with more space in your closet.

6. Revisit your Maybe pile. Go back through it piece by piece, and ask each one, "Why do you deserve a place in my closet?" If there isn't a really good answer, then move it to a new Toss pile. If you have a piece of clothing in the Maybe pile that you hold on to because someone special gave it to you as a gift or used to own it and gave it to you, but you never wear it yourself, put it on, take a picture of yourself in it, and donate it. Now you can have the memory without the clutter.

7. Revisit your Love pile and repeat step 6. Note: If you discover that you don't actually love anything in your Love pile, don't worry, and please don't go out and buy all new items that you think you love. The way you feel about your clothes is going to change from day one to the end of the challenge. I recommend waiting as long as possible to add anything new. Take time to discover what you really want and need in your closet.

8. Move your remaining Maybe pile and Love pile to another room, if they're on your bed. Put anything you're ready to donate in a box, and bring it to a homeless shelter or donation center ASAP. Don't leave it in the trunk of your car for a year.

9. Take a walk or a nap or drink some water. Please don't skip this step. It's important.

10. Clean and wash your empty closet and drawers. Air them out and prepare them for your brand-new tiny wardrobe.

11. Don't worry about the items you still have left. We're working toward 33. If you still have 333, don't panic! We'll get through this.

12. Box up your Maybe pile. Again, don't panic! You aren't giving it away; you're just giving it a break. Box it up and label the box "MAYBE—if I don't miss this, I will donate it at the end of 90 days without looking in the box." Seriously, write that on the box. Put the box in your garage, attic, or any other room besides your closet (preferably somewhere out of sight).

Feeling worried and/or overwhelmed is completely natural at this stage. Everything is going to be okay. This is something new and really different from how you've been living your life, so let me reassure you: You will have enough to wear for any occasion or season with your 33 items. For extra reassurance, remind yourself that at any time, if you don't like dressing with less, you can bring all the crap and chaos back into your closet and your life.

Before moving forward to the really fun part of developing a capsule wardrobe, take one last hard look at your Love pile. Does anything appear less lovely? Do you have a friend who could give you feedback on outfits you try on? If there is anything left that could move to the Maybe or Toss pile, move it.

HOW TO CREATE YOUR PROJECT 333 SEASONAL CAPSULE WARDROBE

Now it's time to put all your hard work into the final step and create your three-month seasonal capsule collection. You should have *all* your clothing, shoes, jewelry, and accessories from every season ready! You'll only be building for a three-month season, but if you have everything out, you can store it by season for easy transition at the end of the challenge. Keep in mind that this is *your* list for *your* wardrobe for *your* life. For inspiration to stop comparing and start wearing clothing that really fits you, listen to the audio recording I made on the Project 333 Resources page here: https://bemorewithless.com /project333-resources.

LET'S MAKE LISTS

If you like lists, you're going to enjoy the next few steps. Start by making a list of categories like this:

- JEWELRY
- ACCESSORIES
- SHOES
- SHIRTS

- PANTS
- SKIRTS
- DRESSES
- OUTERWEAR

Estimate how many items you'll need in each category. Play around with these numbers, and expect to change them up as you finalize your list. It's sort of like creating a budget for your monthly expenses: It rarely works the first time. Your numbers should add up to 33 or less.

Next, you'll be identifying the core items and foundation of your wardrobe. These are the items that you know will make the final list of 33 items and will probably be included on each of your lists throughout the year if you continue to dress with less. There are certain items you use every day or nearly every day. Make a list of those items. There is more than one way to approach this, but I start like this . . .

CORE (NONCLOTHING) ITEMS. These are pieces I use on a regular basis:

1. sunglasses
2. purse
3. workbag
4. necklace
5. bracelet
6. heavy scarf
7. light scarf

Now I know I have 26 items left, so I move to shoes:

8. heels
9. flats
10. boots
11. sneakers/walking shoes

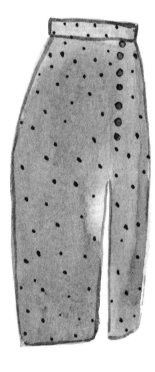

I can add the actual item details later, but this gives me an idea of how many pieces of clothing I'm going to include. Now I know I have 22 items left for clothing. At first that scares the crap out of me, but then I realize I only need a few pairs of pants, a skirt, a dress or three, and then shirts/jackets/outerwear. Summer is much easier because I don't need mittens, a hat, or extra jackets.

CORE CLOTHING ITEMS (THINGS I WEAR ON A REGULAR BASIS). Your list doesn't have to look like mine, but this might help you visualize the process:

12. jeans
13. black T-shirt
14. white button-down shirt
15. blazer

16. zip-up sweatshirt

17. navy dress

I still haven't looked at my pile of clothing choices, but I have identified the foundation of my wardrobe. Next I can add up to an additional 17 items (or less, if I don't feel I need all 17).

FINALIZE YOUR PROJECT 333 CAPSULE WARDROBE

Start by listing your items on a page numbered 1–33, or find a printable version of the Project 333 Quick Start Guide referenced on page 205, here: https://bemorewithless.com/project333 -resources.

You'll be crossing things off and rewriting, and that's okay. Take the pressure off by reminding yourself that this is for three months, not thirty years. Don't worry about picking the perfect items. Perfection is highly overrated, and you're working with pieces you love, so it'll be hard to pick the wrong items.

Start by adding your core items and then fill out your list with additional pieces. Once your list is complete, hang up the items that made the cut and put them away. The rest of your items can stay in a pile. If having clothing everywhere and leaving that pile out in the open is annoying, think about how it would feel if it were gone for good. Don't panic—I said *think* about it. Take a picture of the pile you have left over and then take a picture of your simple, calm, beautiful closet. Breathe.

WHAT ABOUT THE OTHER STUFF?

Okay, you have your 33 items and the stuff you're boxing up to revisit later, but what about the other stuff? Don't forget to be thoughtful about the part of your wardrobe that isn't part of your 33, too. Create as much space as you can to get the full benefit of this minimalist fashion challenge.

> SLEEPWEAR: Remove anything you sleep in from your piles. Make sure you love sleeping in it and then put it away. If you wear your pj's to the store, you have to count them. That's only one of many reasons to stop doing that (winky face).
>
> WORKOUT GEAR: If you run, walk, ski, hike, or play tennis or other sports, you probably have sport-specific clothing. This doesn't count toward your 33. If you stop at the grocery store and have your tennis skirt on, that is okay. If you wake up in the morning and put on your yoga pants to run errands, then you have to count them in your 33. Work out in your workout clothes.
>
> LOUNGEWEAR: If you have clothing that you wear to work in the yard, clean the house, walk the dogs, cuddle up and watch a movie or read a book, or items that you would never wear out of the house, keep them separate from your 33.

Don't overdo it in these categories to make up for the empty space in your closet. Include what you need and nothing more. As you move through a season of Project 333 and are feeling brave, let go of items you aren't using. I drastically reduced the number of items I didn't count in these three categories over my first year of dressing with less. There isn't a specific number of items in any of these categories that is right for everyone. Consider your lifestyle and what you actually use and enjoy. Even more important than choosing clothes that match—sticking with 33 items, and not wearing pj's to the grocery store—is that you please only include clothing that fits *now* and is in good repair. If for some reason, your clothes don't fit during the next three months, feel free to replace or tailor your items. Again, this is not a project in suffering. Project 333 should bring you peace and joy, not frustration!

UNRULY

DOING PROJECT 333 ALREADY MAKES YOU A RULE breaker, so what you find in this chapter shouldn't be a shock to you. You are now a fashion rule breaker, a consumer rule breaker, a marketing rule breaker, and a society rule breaker. Seriously, you're breaking a bunch of rules, both said and unsaid, so don't be afraid to break the rules to make this challenge work for you. I don't want to encourage you to break them, but I'd rather you take the challenge with some broken rules than not take the challenge at all. Project 333 does have rules, and they can help you discover more than you know about what you need and don't need in your closet and your life. These boundaries will be more of a blessing than a sacrifice. That said, if there's something about the challenge rules that completely freaks you out, don't let that be a deal breaker. This is not an all-or-nothing proposition. There are lessons to be learned in even the tiniest steps toward dressing with less. Don't dismiss the whole thing just because there's a small part you don't think you can deal with. I try to remember that when reading books and articles, too. I used to get so annoyed with one small thing I'd read and let that sway my entire opinion of the book or article. Now I break down the bits, and understand that I don't have to accept it all to learn from part of it.

The challenge rules will help, and once you get going, they'll seem way less intimidating than they do now. But maybe you really aren't ready for the whole enchilada. Participants have been breaking rules and modifying Project 333 to better fit their lifestyles since the beginning. Note: "I could never do that" is not a good reason to modify the rules (see chapter six for more on challenging your nevers). Here are a few ways to break the rules.

Get unruly if:

YOU WEAR A UNIFORM TO WORK. If you wear scrubs or another type of uniform to work and need multiples, count all your uniforms as one of your 33 items. I worked in advertising sales, meeting clients, attending community events, and participating in in-office meetings, and had no problem wearing 33 items for work and life. It can be done in most situations, but if you would rather not count additional uniforms, don't.

YOU LOVE JEWELRY. I used to own and wear a bunch of jewelry, but now I only wear a few pieces, and even fewer in the winter (to accommodate a hat, gloves, and an extra scarf in my 33 items). I didn't intend to stop wearing most of my jewelry, but after three months without it, it felt excessive to bring it all back. Wearing it didn't feel like me anymore. I used to buy jewelry to complement my outfits, but now I wear jewelry that means something to me, not because it matches my dress. I recommend putting your jewelry away for the first phase so you can truly determine if you need/want it at all, but if that's a deal breaker, don't count your jewelry at first.

YOU WORRY ABOUT WEATHER CHANGES. If you feel tempted to build in extra pieces for weather, consider packing a small box of extras you can easily access if you need them. I live in Salt Lake City, Utah, and in some seasons, I have to be able to dress for any weather between 0° and 100°F. In fact, my very first Project 333 season started in October 2010, when it was in the nineties, and by the end of the three months, it was snowing. That means there are a few items I wear only in the beginning or end of a season. There is always a tank top and other layering pieces in my collections so I'm never too cold or too hot.

YOU THINK YOU BETTER KEEP SOMETHING "JUST IN CASE." Simply make a "just in case" box. Put all the things in there that you *never* use but might need one day, just in case. Don't list the contents on the box, but label the box "Just in Case." If you remember (without looking) that you need something from your box, get it. Spoiler alert: It probably won't happen.

YOU THINK 33 ITEMS ISN'T ENOUGH. The funny thing is, even though you may have hundreds of items in your closet, you're wearing only a fraction of them. Thirty-three is enough for most of us, but it's also an arbitrary number. If you'd rather do Project 335 or 340, go for it. This experiment will be successful as long as you're testing your limits to understand what "enough" means to you. Don't be surprised if you don't even use all 33 items in three months, though.

Remember, you aren't being graded, and I'm not going to make a surprise visit to your closet. This is just for you! Consider the rules as they are, but know you do have permission to break them. After a modified season (with a few broken rules) of Project 333, consider trying it by the book.

If you broke the rules and still noticed benefits from Project 333, you might have more confidence breaking rules in other areas of your life. What other rules could you break? Don't consider just the written rules, but the unwritten ones, too, the rules and expectations that other people have quietly (or not so quietly) set for you. Maybe it's time to take your life back by breaking all the rules or creating your own.

Remember that this challenge is supposed to make your life better, easier, more enjoyable. If Project 333 is making you cranky or adding more stress to your life, modify the rules, try the challenge another time, or ask for help from a friend you like spending time with. By modifying the rules, you have a chance to experience the benefits, fight your fears, and see for yourself if there's anything to this minimalist fashion project that adds value to your life. If there is, try it again, following a little closer to the original rules. There's no prize for practicing perfectly, so do this in a way that helps you get started. Whatever your approach, make it fun, challenging, and meaningful.

13

FEAR

FEAR ISN'T ALWAYS A BAD THING. SOME FEARS HOLD US
back in a positive way. For instance, if you're hiking and see a
furry spider on the trail, when fear says, "Don't touch that,"
it's helpful. (Yes, this has happened to me, but fear didn't say,
"Don't touch that"—fear said, "Girl, *run*.") Same goes for ven-
omous snakes and other potentially dangerous situations. But
these aren't typically the fears we're dealing with on a daily basis. These aren't the fears that are holding us back from thriving in our own lives, and they certainly aren't the fears that
keep us from trying this fashion challenge. I promise there are
no snakes or spiders involved!

As I overhauled my life and made changes one by one, fear
popped up from inside and outside. I had my own resistance to
change, and people who love me had theirs, too. I had to address my own first. That meant thanking well-meaning friends
and family for their concern, doing it my way, and then circling

back for more meaningful conversations. I couldn't entertain all the fear at once. It would've been debilitating. Here are some of the fears I've seen come up about Project 333, and some bigger fears that we all struggle with.

PROJECT 333 FEARS

These fears come up over and over again, but more from people anticipating the problem and less from people actually experiencing them. Most people don't experience these issues, but it's a good reminder that our anticipation of fear can be just as scary as the thing we fear actually happening. Worse, sometimes, because fear stops us from getting started.

> WEATHER CHANGES. If you're concerned because where you live, it snows at the beginning of spring but it's really warm by the end, I can relate. Choose your 33 items knowing that some of your pieces will be worn only in the very beginning or at the very end of the challenge. I purposely didn't choose three months of similar weather. This is a challenge, after all. If your items don't keep you warm enough or cause you to suffer in some other way due to inclement weather, make adjustments. It's tempting to prepare for every possible circumstance, but it's not realistic. Let go a little and test your fears—you'll become more comfortable with uncertainty when you discover that either what you feared never happened or that you can make a small change and be okay.

LAUNDRY. I don't do any more laundry than I used to, but I do take better care when doing laundry because I want my clothes to last. I wash everything in cold water and line dry it (inside or out) when possible. I also wash everything together—whites, darks, towels . . . all get washed when I have enough of one thing or another to fill the washer. I know, I'm a terrible person.

WORK CHALLENGES. If you dress differently for your job than for the rest of your life, there are a few things you can do to make a capsule wardrobe work. For starters, dress your workwear down about 10 percent and your out-of-work-wear up about 10 percent. No one will notice, and you'll likely be more comfortable everywhere. If you wear a uniform to work, count all your uniforms as one item.

WEIGHT FLUCTUATIONS. If you're used to housing several sizes in your closet to accommodate weight fluctuations, only keeping one size on hand will feel scary. Remember, though, that the challenge is only three months long, and most clothing can accommodate some fluctuation. When you build your Project 333 capsule collection, only include items that fit you today.

While there are others, these are the four big fears about Project 333, and they typically come from people who haven't tried the challenge. They're all imagined problems, for the most part. They haven't happened yet. They may never happen. You can deal with them when they do, if they do. (They probably won't.) When you can see your excuses as things that haven't happened yet, you'll begin to move outside your comfort zone in many other situations, too.

If we zoom out for a minute and look at bigger life changes and what gets in the way of thriving in your own life, you may discover these fears popping up, too.

1. FEAR OF MISSING OUT (FOMO). We struggle with the fear of missing out on activities, information, opportunities, connections, and many other things. We struggle to keep up, to catch up, to be included, noticed, and loved, all in the name of FOMO. With FOMO, you may overcommit or be constantly checking email or social media feeds. You want to be here for your life but also stay connected to and involved with everything else. The simple truth is that you can't be everywhere.

The remedy for FOMO is presence.

When you are truly present, there's no regret about the past or anxiety about the future. When you are present, you notice everything and everyone around you; the big picture, the little pictures, and all the tiny details that contribute to the moments that make up the here and now, that make up your life. And that's just what happens on the outside. When you give yourself permission to be fully alive and aware, your body, heart, and soul change on the inside, too. That's presence. It's not easy. It takes practice, and it's the most effective remedy for FOMO.

2. FEAR OF DISAPPOINTING OTHERS (FODO). This is the fear that makes us say yes when we want to say no. It's the fear that keeps us quiet when we disagree, and it's the fear that leaves us feeling depleted and resentful. People-pleasers especially hate to disappoint others, but the truth is that other people's disappointment has very little to do with you. If someone has expectations of you that don't align with your schedule, your interests, or the expectations you have, they may be disappointed, but since you never set those expectations to begin with, they're not your responsibility. If managing other people's expectations stresses you out, remind yourself that you are not the expectations manager. The only expectations you get to manage are your own. Another important thing to note is that disappointment is survivable.

The remedy for FODO is boundaries.

One way to soften the blow and sometimes avoid disappointment altogether is to be very clear about your boundaries. As author Brené Brown says, "Clear is kind and unclear is unkind." Businesses often have policies to let you know what to expect. People have boundaries. If a business has policies you disagree with, you may stop doing business with them. With people, it's a little different. Often, boundaries are pushed, or not honored. Most will understand, but some won't. A wise person once said, "The people who get upset about you setting boundaries are the ones who were benefiting from you having none." There is always one person who can honor your boundaries, though. It's you. By honoring your boundaries, you remind others that boundaries matter, and you may inspire them to create their own.

3. FEAR OF TRUSTING YOURSELF. If you're afraid or unsure about trusting yourself, it will be almost impossible to remedy FOMO or FODO, because staying present is hard, and creating and enforcing your own boundaries will be very challenging. I can speak to this directly, because there were many years when I didn't know how to trust myself. I looked outward for answers and often second-guessed myself.

If you're running on autopilot, constantly reacting to life's demands and everything thrown your way, you may have forgotten what's best for you. I know I did. I forgot who I was, what I believed, and how to trust myself. I forgot what was best for me. I forgot my heart. Maybe you've forgotten yours, too.

The way to trust yourself is to start listening to your heart. Try this simple heart practice:

STEP 1: Create a little sanctuary where you can sit quietly for 5 minutes a day. This may be as simple as taking a deep breath (wherever you are), in through your nose and out through your mouth (like a really big sigh), to signify the start of your practice. Or if you have a place in your home where you could place a candle, journal, pen, and blanket or other comfort items, do that.

STEP 2: Put your hands on your heart. Sit quietly for 5 minutes. After a few cleansing breaths, in through the nose and out through the mouth (seriously, let it all out), close your eyes or turn your gaze down and focus on your breath. Next, place one hand on your heart and cover it with your other hand. Feel your heart beating. Feel the warmth of your heart and your hands. While continuing to breathe in and out with some intention, simply listen to your heart. Do this every day. Try the practice in silence or with soothing music. For the first few weeks, just show up and listen to your heart. Then start to ask questions or write down what you hear. By showing up for this practice on a consistent basis, you'll begin to remember yourself and what matters to you. You'll learn to trust yourself.

Let go of these fears so you can show all the way up for your life. These fears aren't protecting you. They're dragging you down and holding you back. Letting go of these three fears will take time and practice. Start by noticing the fears as they come up. Respond to the fear of missing out with presence. Respond to the fear of disappointing others by creating boundaries. And respond to the fear of trusting yourself by putting your hands on your heart.

People who haven't tried this fashion challenge often share their fears about it, and people who have tried it share their gratitude. Before I started, I was scared, too, and had lots of questions and excuses, but they all boiled down to me thinking I wouldn't have enough. Fear will tell you that you'll never have enough. When you finish this challenge, you can tell fear that you do. The realization that you need way less than you think to be happy will change your life in the most amazing ways. Instead of judging yourself for having these fears or others, or letting the fears hold you back, acknowledge them, smile, and move forward anyway.

P.S. Important to remember: Laundry and weather are not spiders and snakes.

MESSY

SIMPLICITY IS A POWERFUL PATH FOR SELF-IMPROVEMENT, and Project 333 is a challenge that can make a really big difference on that path. It's been life-changing for me and many others. Thanks to simplicity, I live a healthy life even though I have multiple sclerosis and feel way better than I used to when I was deep in clutter, debt, stress, and wardrobe mess.

PERFECTION HAS NO PLACE HERE

There's no one right way to do this wardrobe challenge, but if your focus is on doing it perfectly, chances are (like other things) you won't do it at all. Give yourself permission to figure things out and have fun along the way. There are rules to help you, but again, not to suggest one best way. I've seen so many different versions of Project 333 wardrobes, and while they're not best for me, they are just right for the people who created them. If you love wearing colorful jackets, patterned shirts, all dresses, no dresses, extra shoes . . . do it. Let it be a little uncertain and a lot messy . . . most things are. If there are one or two outfits in your closet that you really enjoy wearing, create a uniform with your 33 items and wear very similar things each day. Use other examples you might find on the internet for inspiration and experimentation, but give yourself room to be you and decide what you want to wear. If you aren't sure what you want, the only way to figure it out is to start.

I can think of many times I didn't try something because I was afraid I couldn't do it or because I was afraid I wouldn't do it the right way or the best way. That grade-school-report-card mentality stayed with me, and I thought people were still grading me on things like what I did for work, what I wore, where I lived, and how I spent my money. I know it sounds silly, but we all carry a little of that "What will they think of me?" and "How will I measure up to the people around me?" and that's okay. Because even if they *are* thinking about us, that says nothing about us and everything about them, right? I'm guilty of the judgment-making, too, and as soon as I notice I'm caught up in it, I realize it's all about me and my fears and thoughts about myself.

By seeing perfection, judgment, or fear of judgment for what it really is (even though it still trips me up from time to time), I try things even if I don't know how or don't know if they'll work. I turn things upside down, burn them down, build them back up, re-create, reinvent, rewrite, and stumble through until my messy idea turns into a butterfly. The purpose of Project 333 isn't to create a perfect capsule wardrobe; it's to give yourself a little room to breathe. The butterfly of this fashion challenge isn't your clothes. It's you.

LET THINGS BE MESSY

While living a simpler life with less stress can add more health, wealth, and happiness to our lives, it can't prevent every mess. For instance . . .

- Even though my closet is tidy, I still catch colds.
- Even though I'm debt-free, anxiety still gets the best of me.
- Even though my calendar has tons of white space, I still get hurt, inside and out.
- Even though I meditate daily, I still say things I wish I hadn't.
- Even though my home is clutter-free, there are days when I'm a hot mess.
- Even though I live in a small space and run a small business, big emergencies still come up.

We can't simplify our way into a perfect life, nor should we want to. Simplicity is a tool to help us reduce stress and improve our lives, not to control them or convince ourselves we have even the slightest chance of controlling our lives (or the world). I bring it up, though, in case you're just getting started, or struggling, or comparing, or just curious about what life looks like on the other side. I paint a beautiful picture of minimalism and simplifying, but some days, even with simplicity, life is messy. We are messy. It's part of the human condition. Highs, lows, ups, downs . . . all of it comes with being human, even when we've simplified.

I don't have to give my closet much attention anymore, but I have to work on myself every day. Feeling calm and centered doesn't come naturally. I overreact when I want to underreact. I hold on when I mean to let go. In between all the lovely parts are messy parts. Sometimes I think I've got it all together, but unless I'm intentionally focused, I can be all over the place. Living with less, practicing a morning routine, and taking really good care of myself help me be more me. A little bit each day matters more than trying to squeeze it all in over a weekend. Consistency matters more than intensity. It's a day-by-day, inch-by-inch adventure.

Life is messy. Simplicity helps, but it's not a cure-all. We have to keep coming back to ourselves. We have to remember what matters and what we care about. Even when it's hectic or sad or scary out there, we can still be our warm, loving, amazing, gracious selves. Just because things are crazy around you doesn't mean things have to be crazy within you. On the days when you aren't your best and when things are messy, be gentle with yourself. Don't expect or demand more than you have to give. Be patient and remind yourself that things always turn around. Treat yourself like you would treat a really good friend having a bad day. Invite simplicity to improve your life, not to perfect it. Even the messes have something to offer if we're willing to notice the lessons.

Your capsule wardrobe won't be perfect. Do it anyway. Each season, you'll make it a little better. Never perfect, but better. Less perfection equals more happiness, more risk-taking, and better relationships, including the one you have with yourself.

BOREDOM

A BIG CONCERN ABOUT DRESSING WITH 33 ITEMS OR less is boredom. We are afraid that we won't have enough, and that we'll get bored as a result. This is a valid concern if your clothes are the most interesting thing about your life. When I had a closet stuffed with clothes, I was often bored with my wardrobe. I'd flip through my clothes and think, *I have nothing to wear.* I kept buying things to make my wardrobe less boring, and after a successful shopping trip, I'd think I had fixed things. But as soon as the purchase high wore off and I was left a little broker, I'd end up just as bored as I was the last time I needed to get something new. I was looking for that next piece, as if it would fix not just my next look but other things in my life, too. You know, the perfect scarf/belt/jacket to tie the whole look together, to tie everything up in a pretty bow, to complete me. As if the right outfit would make me more interested, or interesting, or complete my life. I was optimistic that something new would settle down any angst or discontent I carried. Of course that never worked.

Despite what you've been conditioned to believe, clothes will not make you a better person. It was a rare moment that I went shopping because I was actually in need. Instead, I purchased clothing to feel better, to be stylish, to look thinner, to feel powerful, to measure up, or to quiet boredom. I wore things to fit in, blend in, and look and try to feel like I belonged in meetings or events (that I never really wanted to be at in the first place). I bought clothing for those reasons and others, always thinking a new pair of shoes or a slimming jacket would help me perform better, look better, feel better, or be better. My purchases did none of those things. Instead, they delivered buyer's remorse, debt, and clutter . . . and then more shopping to feel better. I tried this with things besides clothing, too, but my closet got most of my shopping attention. It took dressing with less to allow me to see my behavior for what it was. Dressing with 33 items or less for years has taught me that there is nothing that will make me better but me.

BACK TO BOREDOM

If you're worried about being bored with a small capsule wardrobe or are currently bored with your big wardrobe, please consider that clothing might not be the issue. Instead of adding one more scarf or pair of shoes or trying a new lipstick color to spice things up, fight boredom with your wardrobe by considering what really interests you and what may actually be boring you. Think about the times you've tried to fix your life by fixing your wardrobe: Did it ever work for very long? Dressing with less provides the time and space, but it's up to you to take the next step and engage in what interests you most. It might not be as easy as shopping, but discovering what really lights you up is going to save you so much heartache.

The next time you feel bored or frustrated with your wardrobe, remind yourself that this feeling probably has nothing to do with your clothes. If you can't figure it out, shift your attention and try one of these suggestions:

33 things you can do when you're bored with your wardrobe:

1. Create a playlist with silly '80s dance tunes . . . and dance.
2. Find a local writing course or book club.
3. Organize a scavenger hunt for your friends.
4. Start a blog.
5. Take a yoga class.
6. Attend a town meeting or community event.
7. Bake for your neighbors.
8. Learn to meditate.
9. Break up with your phone and other digital devices for 24 hours.
10. Create your own 30-day health challenge: quit sugar, become a vegetarian, or drink smoothies every day.

11. Get a massage.
12. Read *Soulful Simplicity*.
13. Grow an herb garden with basil, oregano, and rosemary.
14. Try a new recipe.
15. Visit a new city (or get lost in your own).
16. Read *Man's Search for Meaning*.
17. Take a long walk.
18. Listen to a podcast that features inspiring interviews.
19. Volunteer at a local homeless shelter.
20. Donate your time, talent, or treasure to a charity that matters to you.
21. Give away 25 things that don't matter to you.
22. Smile and say hello to every person you pass for 48 hours.
23. Take yourself out to lunch. Yes, alone.
24. Read *What Should I Do with My Life?*
25. Pull the plug on cable, Hulu, Netflix, etc., for a week or longer.
26. Cancel two appointments that aren't important to you.
27. Walk through a museum.
28. Read *How to Live a Good Life*.
29. Donate your books to a local retirement home.
30. Turn inspiration into action and bring a crazy idea to life.
31. Make a list of 84 things you love.

32. Create a meaningful morning routine.
33. Send a love letter (not through email—use a pen, paper, and stamp).

The problem is not the number of items in your closet but where you choose to direct your attention. Take action with an idea from this list, or make your own list. If you use shopping as an escape from boredom, these 33 suggestions work well for that, too. You'll notice less boredom in your wardrobe when you invest your time, money, and energy doing things that light you up.

Here's a radical idea: Another thing you could do with your boredom is sit with it. I know sitting with feelings and emotions instead of fixing them sounds unreasonable and overwhelming, but sometimes that's all they ask of you. When you're sad, be sad. When you're frustrated, be frustrated. When you're bored, be bored. This too shall pass.

CAPSULE

YOU MAY OR MAY NOT CONTINUE THIS MINIMALIST fashion challenge after the first three months, but either way, consider using the Project 333 rules to create seasonal capsule collections. For your first season of Project 333, I recommend focusing on only the three months ahead of you instead of worrying about future seasons or what the big picture is. You're going to learn new things about yourself and your fashion choices, so what may be true for you at the beginning of the challenge will likely have changed by the end of it. Wait until you know more before making long-term wardrobe decisions.

Following the Project 333 rules (or creating a modified version) is a great way to create a capsule wardrobe, but there are other ways, too. Becca Shern, a registered dietician and the creator of minimalwellness.com, uses the Triple M approach:

> I had no idea what "my style" was, and I frequently felt ambivalent about many of the items in my closet. In fact, I

didn't love the majority of my clothes, but because they were trendy or because they matched the image of what I thought I should wear, I purchased them. I also owned many pieces of clothing that were ill-fitting. Thanks to residual tendencies from my youth, my threads tended to be too large and loose. Being honest with myself about how often I wore a particular item, how it made me feel, or how it looked, and then being ruthless about letting items go that I wasn't wearing or didn't work with my aesthetic, helped dial in my wardrobe. As I was paring down, I homed in on the appropriate sizes, shapes, and styles for my body. My resulting clothes feel far better on, and I look better in them, which improves my self-confidence—

something most of us benefit from. Of course, everyone's individual style will be different, and our styles are likely to shift over time, but my current style is modern, monochrome, and multifunctional (Triple M).

I've found that having a Triple M wardrobe is ideal for my lifestyle— almost every piece of clothing I own can be worn in different ways; has a clean, modern aesthetic; and is either white, gray, or black. Having a simple theme to my clothes means I don't waste time or mental energy deciding if things match—I already know that they do. Because everything goes together, there are innumerable ways I can pull together an outfit, which makes it seem like I have considerably more clothes than I do. For example, I own two pairs of jeans—one dark blue, the other black—and both work well dressed up or down. I also have a couple of different pairs of leggings that I happily wear working out, as long underwear in the winter, or as everyday pants (I love that the activewear trend is growing, not fading). Many of my shirts fit the same description—they can be dressed up or down and can also be worn during workouts. One other key aspect to my clothing selection is quality. In the past, my closet and drawers were filled with inexpensive pieces that were designed for one micro-season, not for years of use. Unsurprisingly, these items rarely fit well and often fell apart, shrank, or wore poorly (hello, pilling). By wearing high-quality, durable, and multifunctional pieces, I save money and mental energy, reduce my environmental impact, and look good in the process.

Men and women (and children) from around the world, with different lifestyles, ages, careers, and body shapes have used Project 333 to create their capsule wardrobes. Some continue to count their items, but not all of them. Visit the Project 333 Resources page (https://bemorewithless.com/project333 -resources) for links to Instagram accounts and blogs to see what other people are including in their Project 333 wardrobes.

Once you hang your new capsule wardrobe in your closet, you can say good-bye to analysis paralysis, running late, and wasted time at the mall, and say hello to saving money, getting dressed with ease, and discovering what's really important to you. If you aren't quite ready to jump into a capsule wardrobe, here are a few ways to test the waters. These ideas will help you begin to experience dressing with less and perhaps create some momentum and confidence for the next step. If you're lost in closet chaos, it may feel overwhelming to start paring back, but these capsule wardrobe tips will help.

1. ELIMINATE ACCESSORIES. Instead of trying to figure out what scarves, handbags, jewelry, or other things you accessorize with to include, eliminate them all, or all but one. This may not be a permanent step, but removing the accessory decision-making process for a few months will help you experience the benefits of dressing with less without struggling to choose.

2. WEAR YOUR FAVORITE COLORS. If you love wearing blue but have a few red items in your wardrobe to "mix things up" or because red was the color of the month in your favorite fashion magazine, let yourself off the hook. You don't have to dress in seasonal colors or colors you think you're supposed to wear. Remove the colors or patterns you don't feel good in for a while.

3. KEEP IT ALL IN ONE PLACE. I used to have clothes and other wardrobe items in different drawers, closets, and storage bins so I never really understood how much I really had. Get all your stuff in one place and then divide it into the stuff you're actually wearing

and enjoying and the stuff you aren't. There's no reason to be sifting through what you don't wear to find what you want to wear.

4. IDENTIFY FIVE FAVORITE OUTFITS. Statistics show we wear 20 percent of our clothes 80 percent of the time, but we still show up and ask, "What am I going to wear?" every morning. Instead, photograph yourself in your five favorite outfits; before you look in your closet, choose from your favorite looks first.

5. GET RID OF THE TAGS. If there are things in your closet with the tags still attached, remove the tags and the items. Give them away, consign them, or sell them. The tags may not seem harmful, but seeing those items every day is a stressful reminder of impulse shopping, overspending, and bad purchase decisions.

6. ONLY KEEP ONE SIZE IN YOUR CLOSET. Multiple sizes may feel like a safety net, but they may also be a painful reminder of how you feel in your own skin. There's no proof that smaller sizes encourage you to lose weight. Only keep clothes in your closet that fit your body.

7. LET GO OF THE GUILT. Closets are full of emotions, with guilt often at the top of the list. Guilt for spending too much, for not wearing what you have, for clothes fitting poorly, and for not enjoying pieces other people have given you. Unfortunately, the guilt is completely unproductive. Take a look through your closet and pull out anything that makes you feel

guilty. Box it up and revisit it in three months. If you don't love it by then or it still makes you feel bad, give it away. While you're at it, consider the guilt you're holding on to in other areas of your home and life, and let that go too.

8. ADD MUSIC. Instead of continually adding new pieces to your wardrobe because they're on sale, or because you need a lift from shopping, or whatever excuse you're using to justify buying something new, add music. Create a playlist of ten songs that make you smile, and when you feel the urge to shop, turn the music on instead. Those ten songs will lift you up, and the time that passes while you're listening will be enough of a delay to ease your mind and distract you from shopping. Check out my ten songs on the Project 333 Resources page: https://bemorewithless .com/project333-resources.

9. ASK A FRIEND FOR HELP. Invite someone who isn't emotionally attached to your stuff to go through your clothes with you. Trust them to help you let go.

10. DON'T BUY YOUR CAPSULE WARDROBE. You could go out and buy 33 "perfect pieces," but then you'll end up spending money you might not have on things that you may not love in three months. Instead, figure out what you really need by working with what you have. If you need to add a piece or two, do it, but otherwise, give yourself three months of dressing with what you

have to better understand what you need for a capsule wardrobe that works best for you.

CAPSULE WARDROBE TRANSITIONS

Depending on where you live, you may need one or more capsule collections to accommodate different weather and seasons. A Project 333 capsule wardrobe is built for three months. I create four seasonal capsule wardrobes a year. People often assume that means I have 132 items (4 × 33) for the year, but I actually have fewer pieces. Here's what it looks like when I move from one Project 333 season to the next.

At the end of my winter season (January through March), I remove all the items I won't use in the spring. What's left is more than half my collection. These are the pieces from my winter collection that are in my spring collection, too:

1. small purse
2. laptop bag
3. sunglasses
4. bracelet
5. necklace
6. scarf
7. shoes—black flats
8. shoes—black heels
9. shoes—walking
10. jeans
11. black skirt

12. navy dress
13. black tank top
14. white button-down shirt
15. black long-sleeved shirt
16. black/gray shirt
17. black sweatshirt
18. navy blazer

Most of those items will move into my summer and fall collections, too. Project 333 is not an invitation to create a brand-new wardrobe every three months.

If you're worried about fluctuating weather conditions during a certain season, remember that you won't be able to wear your entire collection all season. Build in a few pieces for the beginning when temps are cooler or warmer and another few pieces for the end of the season when the weather is likely the complete opposite of where it started. More than half my collection is in play for six months or longer. When you're building new capsule collections, assess the items from the previous season and find crossover pieces. If you do that each season, you can gradually reduce the size of your overall wardrobe and experience more benefits of Project 333.

ERIN (WINTER)

name : Verena (Erin) Polowy

city : Edmonton, Alberta, Canada

capsule colors : Gray, navy, dark red, beige

capsule basics : Sweaters, jeans, boots, and tees

favorite outfit : In winter, I love keeping it simple and just wearing my comfy, stretchy black pants, with a thick, cozy sweater and a pair of boots.

instagram : @verenaerin

website : https://verenaerin.ca

TO SHARE HER PASSION ABOUT SUSTAINABLE STYLE, Erin runs a YouTube channel, My Green Closet (https://www.youtube.com/user/MyGreenCloset), where she creates videos about eco and ethical fashion, capsule wardrobes, natural beauty, minimalism, what's happening in the fashion industry, and tips for living more consciously. Erin's been sharing her Project 333 wardrobe online for years, and I'm happy to introduce you to her.

Q: TELL US A LITTLE BIT ABOUT YOURSELF.

A: I have a background in fashion design and love clothing, so most people are surprised to learn that I have such a small wardrobe. Sustainability is incredibly important to me, and having a capsule wardrobe has been an amazing tool to allow me to reduce my impact not only through consuming less and producing

less waste but by being able to invest in brands that manufacture in a sustainable and ethical way. I'm Canadian and just moved back to a very cold part of Canada after living in Germany for more than three years, so my capsule wardrobe has had to adapt to a few different climates since I started it. I work as a blogger, YouTuber, and consultant.

Q: HOW DID YOU LEARN ABOUT PROJECT 333?

A: I began this journey because of a growing desire to live and consume more consciously. I was horrified by the environmental and ethical impacts of the fashion industry in particular, and knew I had to change my fast-fashion shopping habits. I wanted to invest in better-quality pieces and support brands that aligned with my values. As I slowly started to do this, I came across the concept of a capsule wardrobe and it seemed like a great solution—a small, well-curated wardrobe that would allow me to focus on quality over quantity but still give me a way to create a lot of different outfit combinations. Looking more into capsule wardrobes, I came across Project 333, and it felt like the perfect way to try it out and give my wardrobe and shopping habits a "reset." I challenged myself to try it for a year, and now, four-plus years later, I can't imagine going back.

Q: WHAT HAVE YOU LEARNED FROM DRESSING WITH A CAPSULE WARDROBE?

A: The biggest thing I've learned is that I don't need a huge wardrobe to feel good or have fun with clothing and style. I love that I can reach into my closet and put something together with no thought, and having a small wardrobe has pushed me to experiment with how I wear and combine pieces if I want to get creative. I've discovered so many outfits that I love but would likely never have tried together if I had a huge closet. A capsule wardrobe focuses on the clothes you feel good in and love wearing, so you learn a lot about your style, and it allows you to let go of all the pieces that just bring up guilt and negative feelings. My wardrobe now feels like a clean space full of pieces I love, instead of a chaotic space that just caused stress and guilt.

It also means so much to me that my wardrobe reflects both my personal style and my sustainable and ethical values, and because I'm buying so much less, I can invest more in responsible brands, and that feels wonderful.

Q: WHAT ADVICE WOULD YOU GIVE TO SOMEONE STARTING PROJECT 333 OR A CAPSULE WARDROBE TODAY?

A: It's a learning process, so don't expect everything to work right away, and also don't be hard on yourself if it doesn't go as you expected. Through wearing your capsule, you'll learn a lot about your personal style and what actually does and doesn't work for your lifestyle. Each season you can incorporate the things you've learned into building your next capsule; over time, it gets easier, and you'll also have a better sense of the pieces and outfits you most like to wear.

Also, don't get too caught up in the "rules"—if something doesn't work, swap it or feel free to make adjustments. Remember that your capsule wardrobe is a tool for you to use, so it has to work for you!

Q: AS YOU'VE SHIFTED YOUR FOCUS AWAY FROM ADDING TO YOUR WARDROBE, HAVE YOU HAD MORE RESOURCES (TIME/MONEY/ENERGY) FOR OTHER PASSIONS?

A: Before my capsule I spent so much time shopping just for fun, and shifting that to other activities I enjoy has been wonderful. My capsule wardrobe also was part of a greater journey to slow down and focus on what's most important in my life. I've been able to build a career around something I'm incredibly passionate about, and through generally buying less and living more minimally, my husband and I have more time and money to spend on traveling and other experiences, which has been incredible and is something I'm so grateful for.

Erin's Winter Project 333 List

1. striped oversize button-down shirt
2. long blue/gray shirt
3. dark gray linen V-neck tee
4. navy scoop-neck tee
5. maroon-and-white-checked tunic
6. dark gray/blue velvet bodysuit
7. gray knit top
8. dark gray/brown V-neck sweater
9. dark red sweater
10. white Icelandic sweater
11. light gray sweater
12. dark bootcut jeans
13. dark brown wool pants
14. black skinny knit pants
15. linen navy midi skirt
16. gray knit short skirt
17. beige cardigan
18. black-checked drapey cardigan

19. gray oversize jacket

20. red/navy wool coat

21. black long-sleeved dress

22. wool draped dress

23. gray T-shirt dress

24. beige purse

25. gray backpack

26. cream knit beret

27. blue cable-knit beanie

28. knit color-blocked scarf

29. paisley blanket scarf

30. blue mittens

31. blue snow boots

32. burgundy heeled boots

33. light brown low boots

CHRISTINE (SPRING)

name : Christine A. Platt

city : Washington, DC

capsule colors : Black, denim, pops of color

capsule basics : Jumpsuit/rompers, denim jacket, skinny jeans

favorite outfit : Red jumpsuit

instagram : @afrominimalist

website : theafrominimalist.com

I FOUND CHRISTINE WHILE SEARCHING #PROJECT333 on Instagram and fell in love with her and the images and messages she was sharing on Instagram. I also appreciated that someone living in a fast-paced city like Washington, DC, was willing to take on a slow-fashion challenge.

Q: TELL US A LITTLE BIT ABOUT YOURSELF.

A: As a scholar of African and African-American history and culture, I have such love, respect, and appreciation for literature. There is so much power in the written word. Through divine providence, my commitment to capturing and preserving the

history of the African diaspora manifested into a career as an author and storyteller. I write historical fiction and nonfiction for people of all ages (although I have a special affinity for young audiences). Writing is definitely my calling. I love what I do so much! I'm also the mother to my amazing teenage daughter, Nalah, who is a classically trained violinist, visual artist, and creative writer. We were made for each other, obviously. *smile*

Q: HOW DID YOU LEARN ABOUT PROJECT 333?

A: I learned about Project 333 by divine intervention! I was in the process of becoming a minimalist—downsizing from a large home to a 630-square-foot condo. Naturally, decluttering my closet was a part of the process. I came across Project 333 during one of my "minimalist closet solutions" searches. And it changed my life!

Q: WHAT HAVE YOU LEARNED FROM DRESSING WITH A CAPSULE WARDROBE?

A: Initially, paring down my wardrobe to just a few items sounded daunting. But what I quickly came to realize is that I naturally gravitated toward the same "go-to" pieces and "tried-and-true" ensembles. By being intentional with my "favorites," I was able to really structure my wardrobe in a way that (1) made getting ready for work or play easy, and (2) ensured I'd always love whatever I was wearing.

Q: WHAT ADVICE WOULD YOU GIVE TO SOMEONE STARTING PROJECT 333 OR A CAPSULE WARDROBE TODAY?

A: Start slow, and don't be too hard on yourself. It took me a couple of seasons to really get the hang of things. Also, every so often, take a peek at #project333 on Instagram. It's a great place to get ideas.

Q: AS YOU'VE SHIFTED YOUR FOCUS AWAY FROM ADDING TO YOUR WARDROBE, HAVE YOU HAD MORE RESOURCES (TIME/MONEY/ENERGY) FOR OTHER PASSIONS?

A: Yes! I regained so much time, especially in the mornings, because I'm not standing in front of my closet wondering, *What am I going to wear?* This additional time has been allocated in many ways—writing, yoga/meditation, or simply staying in bed longer and daydreaming. Also, I continuously save money because having a capsule wardrobe forces me to be intentional with every purchase. I really, really have to love something to buy it (and switch it out with something I already own and really, really love!).

Christine's Spring Project 333 List

1. white T-shirt
2. black T-shirt
3. navy-and-white-striped T-shirt
4. white collared shirt
5. denim collared shirt
6. denim jacket
7. red jumpsuit
8. white jumpsuit
9. tan jumpsuit
10. denim jumpsuit
11. boyfriend jeans
12. skinny jeans
13. fitted cropped black pants
14. wide-leg black pants
15. black evening dress (cocktail)
16. colorful/fun formal dress
17. colorful/fun everyday dress
18. denim dress
19. black blazer
20. denim/light blue blazer
21. multicolored blazer
22. weekend/errand dress (T-shirt style or maxi)

23. black loafers/flats
24. white sneakers
25. neutral sandals (low heel or wedge)
26. black sandals (low heel or wedge)
27. black heels/pumps
28. diamond studs
29. silver studs
30. gold hoops
31. silver hoops
32. everyday necklace with gold and silver charms
33. multicolored scarf

ANUSCHKA (SUMMER)

name: Anuschka Rees

city: Berlin, Germany

capsule colors: White, red, peach, yellow, and cream

capsule basics: White cotton shorts, cream A-line skirt, white-and-black-striped bodysuit

favorite outfit: rainbow-striped skirt + red wrap top + light green sandals

instagram: @anuschkarees

website: anuschkarees.com

ANUSCHKA IS THE AUTHOR OF *THE CURATED CLOSET* and *Beyond Beautiful.* Her take on fashion and how we should dress ourselves resonates with me: "Here's the thing: Particularly in recent years we have all been so inundated with typology-based advice, from various fruit-inspired body shape theories to super-in-depth color-analysis quizzes, that the idea that only a small set of clothes and colors works for each person has become widely accepted. And that's pretty sad, I think. Sure, there may be a handful of colors that each one of us looks a little more tired in and a few that we look a little better in, but the vast majority of shades will look just fine. The same goes for shapes/silhouettes: Yes, a few extreme cuts may make you look a little more bottom-heavy or perhaps two pounds lighter, but your body is what it is, and clothes won't magically change that. If something is your style and you love it, I believe you should wear it, regardless of whether it supposedly 'flatters' your body or doesn't. Plus, if we're being honest, 'to flatter' almost always means 'makes you look thinner,' and that definitely shouldn't be your prime objective when it comes to getting dressed."

Q: TELL US A LITTLE BIT
ABOUT YOURSELF.

A: I'm a hard-core introvert. If it weren't for my boyfriend, who drags me out to social events periodically, I would spend all day writing and hanging out with my cats and books.

Q: WHAT'S BEEN THE MOST IMPORTANT THING YOU'VE LEARNED FROM DRESSING WITH LESS?

A: It's okay to ignore "fashion rules." When you start to be more selective when it comes to shopping, you quickly learn to distinguish between things you actually, truly like and clothes you primarily wear because someone told you they're flattering or trendy.

Q: WHAT ADVICE WOULD YOU GIVE TO SOMEONE STARTING PROJECT 333 OR A CAPSULE WARDROBE TODAY?

A: Don't aim for perfection or getting it 100 percent right. The whole point of this is to make your life easier, save you time, and de-stress your experience with clothes. So please don't fret too much about details or stress about choosing the optimal combination of clothes. It's okay to not look polished to perfection 24/7.

Q: AS YOU'VE SHIFTED YOUR FOCUS AWAY FROM ADDING TO YOUR WARDROBE, HAVE YOU HAD MORE RESOURCES (TIME/MONEY/ENERGY) FOR OTHER PASSIONS?

A: Definitely! I used to use fashion and shopping as a creative outlet, and I used to go shopping all the time. Nowadays, I put my creative energy into my writing, and I even took up painting, because I've realized I love playing around with colors.

Anuschka's Summer Project 333 List

1. small red cross-body bag
2. basket bag
3. white clutch
4. cream sneakers
5. light green sandals
6. white slippers with an exposed heel
7. black Arizona Birkenstocks
8. black heeled sandals
9. sunglasses
10. thin brown belt
11. white cotton shorts
12. light-wash denim shorts

13. gingham shorts
14. wide-leg striped pants
15. red midi skirt
16. striped midi skirt
17. cream A-line miniskirt
18. rust-orange denim miniskirt
19. white sleeveless shirt dress
20. cream/white floral minidress
21. light-wash jean jacket
22. light gray crew-neck T-shirt
23. long-sleeved white linen shirt
24. white camisole
25. cream sleeveless linen shirt

26. khaki linen
    camisole
27. peach camisole
28. medium-blue short-
    sleeved shirt
29. green camisole
30. light yellow T-shirt
31. red wrap top
32. white-and-black-
    striped bodysuit

CAROLINE (FALL)

name : Caroline Joy Rector

city : Dallas, Texas

capsule colors : Cream, nude, rust, honey, brown

capsule basics : Vintage Levi's, oversize sweaters, printed dresses, mules, white sneakers

favorite outfit : Light brown woven mules, vintage Levi's, nude detailed camisole

instagram : @caroline_joy

website : un-fancy.com

CAROLINE SHARES HER CAPSULE WARDROBE JOURNEY, daily outfits, and wardrobe lessons on her website, un-fancy.com. She says, "At the end of my yearlong capsule experiment, I found myself more content, more confident, and more in-tune with my personal style than ever before." She also hosts the Instagram-famous 10x10 Challenge. I asked her to tell us about it: "The 10x10 is a community-driven Instagram challenge. My friend Lee Vosburgh created it to allow people to test out minimalism without a long-term commitment. Simply put, you pick 10 items of clothing from your closet. Include tops, bottoms, and shoes for your everyday life. Don't include accessories, outerwear, underwear, bags, pj's, or gym clothes—they can flow in and out freely. Then, for 10 days, create a new outfit each day using your 10 items. You can do it anytime you want, you can go it alone or grab some friends to join you—it can be whatever you want it to be."

Q: WILL YOU PLEASE TELL US A LITTLE ABOUT YOURSELF?

A: I grew up in a small town in West Texas and was a wedding photographer for seven years before I became a blogger. I've been blogging since 2014 and love it. Aesthetics really speak to me, and along with personal style, I also really enjoy interior design. I love combining vintage with new and enjoy the process of getting that balance just right.

Q: WHAT HAVE YOU LEARNED FROM DRESSING WITH A CAPSULE WARDROBE?

A: I learned that any task is more manageable when you shrink it. For example, I wanted to find my style and revamp my wardrobe, but it felt like too large a task until I shrunk it down to a capsule. Once I put limits on myself, I felt my creativity thrive. I apply this to all areas of life now. If something's feeling overwhelming, I ask myself how I can shrink it.

Q: WHAT ADVICE WOULD YOU GIVE TO SOMEONE STARTING PROJECT 333 OR A CAPSULE WARDROBE TODAY?

A: Don't take it too seriously. The fun of it is in the process and the evolution. When I put together my first capsule wardrobe six years ago, I expected I'd create this one perfect wardrobe and be pretty much set for life. I held on to that ideal a little too tightly, feeling guilty if I needed or wanted new clothes. But life is always changing (whether it's a change in job, lifestyle, body, health, location, etc.). I found that it's refreshing and liberating to accept my life for what it is each day as it changes, without getting fixated on labels or caught up in the mind-set of identity. It's the subtle values within minimalism—curiosity, lifelong learning, gentle mindfulness—that I love more than the label itself. Be gentle with yourself, release labels, and enjoy the journey.

And! If you're trying to abstain from shopping for a little while, feel free to kindly unfollow anyone on Instagram who might make you want to shop a lot, and unsubscribe from retailer newsletters.

Q: AS YOU'VE SHIFTED YOUR FOCUS AWAY FROM ADDING TO YOUR WARDROBE, HAVE YOU HAD MORE RESOURCES (TIME/MONEY/ENERGY) FOR OTHER PASSIONS?

A: I have to laugh here, because a minimal, well-planned wardrobe can certainly free up time, money, and energy for other passions, but since I decided to start a blog about my wardrobe, I've actually devoted *more* time and energy toward my personal style. However, I do find that keeping a curated wardrobe allows me to get lots of time back when choosing outfits each day. It's made the process of getting dressed a lot more enjoyable and fun. It also taught me to be more intentional with my purchases.

And I have to say, the whole process of becoming more intentional about my wardrobe has helped me realize just how much I actually do love style and fashion. It's become a passion for me. Now I get so much joy out of this personal art form!

Caroline's Fall Project 333 List

1. white sneakers
2. light brown woven mules
3. nude lace-up booties
4. brown ankle booties
5. oversize khaki trench coat
6. rust linen trench jacket
7. light-wash high-rise baggy vintage blue jeans
8. black high-rise skinny jeans
9. cream high-rise wide-leg jeans
10. brown polka-dot midi skirt
11. khaki high-rise wide-leg corduroy pants
12. rust floral-print short-sleeved midi dress
13. rust floral-print long-sleeved minidress

14. sleeveless cream midi sweater dress
15. black-and-white-print long-sleeved midi dress
16. cognac plain leather tote
17. rust dressy purse with chain strap
18. nude mini cross-body bag
19. tortoiseshell retro '90s sunglasses
20. small cream hoop earrings
21. delicate gold necklace
22. gold pendant necklace
23. cream sweater with eyelet detailing
24. rust chunky knit sweater
25. taupe oversize sweater
26. sienna chunky-knit cardigan
27. nude detailed camisole
28. white boxy tee
29. ecru soft tee
30. ecru plain soft sweatshirt
31. rust wrap top
32. mustard floral top
33. cream fitted long-sleeved ribbed top

YOU

I SHARED THOSE EXAMPLES OF INSPIRING WOMEN and their Project 333 wardrobes not as a prescriptive but to get you thinking about what will work best for you. What do you want to include in your wardrobe? This may be the first time in your adult life that someone has asked you that question, or that you've asked yourself that question. Typically we wear what everyone else tells us to wear, even if we aren't completely aware we're being told what to wear. We're influenced by what magazines recommend, what trends suggest, and of course those irresistible deals that arrive in our inboxes on a regular basis. It may seem impossible, but if you can break away from what you think you're supposed to wear and consider what you really *want* to wear, eventually you'll create a wardrobe that supports the way you want to live. When you see what a big difference choosing your own wardrobe can make, you'll start questioning the basis of your other life choices. When I say that this is the fashion challenge that is changing closets *and* lives around the world, that's what I mean.

If you're wondering about your personal style, resist trying to identify it before your first season of Project 333. With only 33 items in your closet, you'll begin to think less about what you're wearing and more about who you are and what really fits your body and your lifestyle. That will help you figure out your personal style. It's why I don't recommend buying new clothes to do this fashion challenge. You'll know much more quickly if something is working or not if you're wearing it frequently. My first capsule collection came from items I already owned, and when I put my items together, I threw out all the fashion rules. Today, many years later, my wardrobe is still 33 items or less, but it looks much different than it did ten years ago. It's much less colorful, simpler, and more versatile.

When someone asks me what my personal style is, I say, "It's freedom." I know that's not an appropriate fashion term, but my capsule collection allows me to be free from the rules, free from overspending (time and money) on clothing, free from guilt, free from dressing to impress. My style is freedom.

BACK TO YOU

Project 333 will help you be more you, and it'll also free up some of your resources so you can do a deeper dive into what becoming more you really looks like. Maybe you know exactly who you are, but many of us have experienced a disconnect and are looking for a way back. This isn't about finding yourself. It's about remembering who you are. I'm always learning something new about how simplicity works on my heart, changes my relationships, and influences my work. At first my journey was focused on tasks like decluttering, paying off debt, and downsizing. The changes started on the outside, but the real work was happening on the inside. With each thing, obligation, or assumption I let go of, I remembered who I was. I saw how far I had strayed and made it a priority to come back to myself.

WHY IT'S SO IMPORTANT TO COME BACK TO YOU:

- LIVING OUTSIDE YOURSELF IS EXHAUSTING. IT WILL BREAK YOU DOWN.
- YOU'LL TAKE BETTER CARE OF YOURSELF WHEN YOU ARE MORE YOU.
- YOU'LL GIVE TO THE WORLD IN BIGGER AND BETTER WAYS BECAUSE YOU HAVE AN AUTHENTIC PLACE TO GIVE FROM.
- YOU'LL ATTRACT THE RIGHT PEOPLE FOR YOU. THEY CAN'T KNOW YOU AND LOVE YOU UNTIL YOU DO.
- THERE WILL BE MORE LOVE.

Give yourself all the space, time, and love to come back to who you are. Living with less clutter, busyness, and stress will help you make the room to do what you need to do. Simplifying my life gave me the space, time, and love to be more me, and the following practices led me back. They can lead you back, too.

1. **Write yourself down.**

   In *The Artist's Way*, author Julia Cameron suggests writing three pages every morning, but start with one page, or five minutes, or whatever is approachable for you. Don't edit, judge, or share. Instead, just write yourself down each day. Write about what's on your mind, what made you smile or cry, or what you had for breakfast. Write about your crazy dream, pet peeves—anything you want. It doesn't matter where the commas go, or if your words seem unreasonable, harsh, silly, or angry. Just keep writing down your heart.

   The daily writing helps you notice how you feel, who you are, when you are lost, and when you are found.

2. **Spend time with people who lift you up.**

   Spend time with people who will love you for you. Spend less time with people who won't. Choosing to spend less time with people who sabotage your happiness doesn't mean you can't take time to lift people who can't lift themselves. Give your change, a smile, a sandwich, or a few volunteer hours to people who don't know how to surround themselves with people who lift them. You'll be surprised at how they lift you, too.

Love your people so much, and don't forget to let them love you back.

3. **Stop proving yourself.**

I used to try to prove how good I was at my job by doing more and acting like someone I wasn't. My work wore me down, I got sick a bunch, and I felt completely depleted at the end of every workday, meeting, or event. I never took time to be alone, refuel, or soothe my heart. Instead, I kept pushing and doing more. There was always more to be done, more to prove—bigger goals and higher hoops.

By becoming my work and acting like an extrovert for a really long time, I lost myself. I forgot who I was and what I needed to thrive. I needed some space and breathing room to remember who I was. I had to say, "Enough is enough." I had to be still and listen. Thanks to simplicity, I tapped into the quiet and came back to love. Simplicity soothed the heart of this introvert.

4. **Let go of the excess.**

Keep releasing the excess, the extra, and the stuff that doesn't mean anything to you. For a while, this might mean saying no more than you say yes. It might mean letting people down, spending more time alone, or admitting weakness and asking for help. Take all the time you need, because once you get back to you, you'll be able to give in ways you've never imagined.

5. **Put your hands on your heart.**

   Try the simple heart practice on page 93. Your heart knows who you are—now you just need a little time to know your heart.

6. **Do what's best for you.**

   I draw great inspiration and guidance from hearing other people's stories, talking to friends, and listening to advice, but when I want to know what's best for me, I put my hands on my heart and turn to the person who knows me best. The more you remember and connect with who you are, the more you'll trust yourself to know what's best for you. Your heart knows.

   The more me I am, the easier it is to know what's right for me, who is right for me, and how I can serve the world and live a life of purpose and passion. When I am the most me I can be, my relationships are stronger, my work is better, and I feel more at ease. Forgetting who you are and living outside yourself, outside your heart, is exhausting. Do whatever it takes to come back and be more you.

WHY I DON'T TELL YOU WHAT I'M WEARING

Dressing and living with less is a great way to improve our lives. Project 333 is a simple invitation to dress with less, and because less looks different for everyone, I don't tell you what I'm wearing. While I do share pictures and videos of me and my wardrobe, I'll never tell you the brands I'm wearing, share where I shop, or make recommendations about what you should wear or where you should shop.

Pre-Project 333, there were so many times I bought something because someone recommended it, and then felt disappointed that it didn't work for my body or life. I could have created the Project 333 challenge and my entire business around fashion recommendations and to promote brands and clothing and earn money while you fill your closet with things that I like, but Project 333 isn't about telling you what to wear or encouraging you to shop. I want to work with you, but not like that. I intentionally chose a different message and business model be-

cause I wanted to do something we would both feel good about. I don't think there is a piece of clothing out there that is so special that everyone would benefit from owning it. You have to discover what works best for you. That will take some experimenting, but you'll figure it out and be happier as a result. I don't want to help you find the perfect things to buy. I want to help you be you and wear what best suits you being you. That's when you'll be your happiest and healthiest. It's when you'll most enjoy your life. That's much more exciting to me than helping you create the perfect wardrobe.

If you want to inspire people with your Project 333 lists, you can find Instagram Story templates and other downloadable forms on the Project 333 Resources page.

Let's make this about you.

CREATIVITY

MY HOME IS SIMPLE. MY WARDROBE IS NEUTRAL AND MY calendar is often empty, but my life is full of color, adventure, creativity, and love. That's not the way it always was, though. I used to go out of my way to buy colorful clothing because I thought I was supposed to. I'm sure I'm not the only person who has stood in a department store determined not to buy another black dress, shirt, or pair of pants. I was a little worried that if I couldn't express my creativity through my clothing, I would be less creative in life. Instead, I've discovered the complete opposite. Because I've eliminated all the choices and stopped pouring all my creative energy into getting dressed, I've become more creative in every other area of my life.

Even when we don't consider ourselves artists, I think we all have a deep desire to create and to be creative. If you've ever been moved by a book, brought to tears by a painting or photograph, gotten goose bumps hearing a song for the first time, or tasted a culinary masterpiece, you know there is more than sheer talent behind each creation. There is something majestic, something bigger. You feel it, and the maker feels it. As children we may have been more naturally creative, and I think that's because no one was telling us we couldn't do it. I remember getting a low grade on a drawing of a Main Street shop in the fifth grade and thinking, *I suck at drawing.* Years later, I went to art school, and I still love drawing, painting, photography, writing,

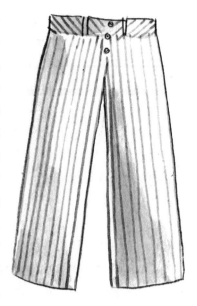

and all things creative. For a while I shut it all down in the name of being an adult. I did work that made money to pay my bills and got all wrapped up in responsibility and obligation. As I began to let go and make more room in my life, I started actively creating again.

Sometimes we can make our lives and schedules more conducive to creating, but other times it just happens. Our creative energy builds, and at some point it has to come out. Expressing ourselves creatively is important. If you're the creative type, there are things you can do to encourage creative flow, but there are also times when creativity dictates the when/how/where/what. When that happens, listen. For me, that often comes when I'm lazily stretching out on my yoga mat or working out and in the thirty seconds just before I start drifting off to sleep. I get the best ideas in the shower, too, or while taking a walk. The last thing I want to do is take all that creative energy and use it to add layers of accessories and color to my outfit. Now, there *is* an exception: fashion designers and people who make clothes, jewelry, accessories—perhaps fashion is your creative outlet or career. Otherwise, I think we spend way too much of our creativity getting dressed. We have more meaningful things to make. Let's not make ourselves busier and more distracted doing things that don't need our attention.

In her beautiful TED Talk "Creative Genius," author Elizabeth Gilbert talks about how past civilizations believed that magical divine entities invisibly assist artists. In her talk, she describes a conversation she had with American poet Ruth Stone, who told Gilbert that when she was growing up in Virginia, she would be working in the fields and she would feel and hear a poem coming at her from over the landscape. When she felt it coming, she knew she had only one thing to do, and that was "run like hell." She would run like hell to the house and she'd be getting chased by this poem and she had to get to a pencil and paper fast enough so that when it thundered through her, she could collect it. If you've ever had a creative idea "thunder through" you, you know you want it to happen again. I think the thundering happens more often than we might imagine, but we miss it, because we're too busy paying attention to the things we think are supposed to matter. By simplifying our wardrobes and our lives, we can listen and respond when creativity calls. We can make space for our craft and creativity whether it be a career, a calling, or just for sheer joy.

So, what do you want to create? What do you want to make? What's waiting inside of you? Is it a book, a batch of incredible vegan cupcakes, a song? Please make it. We need you to make it.

THREE IMPORTANT REASONS TO BE MORE CREATIVE . . .

CREATIVITY PREDICTS A LONGER LIFE. In a *Scientific American* article, "researchers found that only creativity—not intelligence or overall openness—decreased mortality risk. One possible reason creativity is protective of health is because it draws on a variety of neural networks within the brain." Not only can being creative help you live longer, but it can improve your health and quality of life, too.

SOLVE PROBLEMS. Being creative helps you become a better problem-solver in all areas of your life and work. Instead of coming from a linear, logical approach, your creative side can approach a situation from all angles. Creativity helps you see things differently and better deal with uncertainty. Studies show that creative people are better able to live with uncertainty because they can adapt their thinking to allow for the flow of the unknown.

DEVELOP CONFIDENCE. Being creative comes with many ups and downs and a high risk of failure. You have to be vulnerable to share your art, and be willing to take the risk that what you create may never see the light of day. Engaging in the creative process is a great confidence builder, because you discover that failure is part of the process. Once we see failure as something that is survivable, and something that helps us grow and makes our work better, we can release the fear and try new things, even at the risk of failing.

Don't worry about doing creativity wrong. Don't wait until you know it all or have it all. Just ease in, pay attention to thundering ideas, and take advantage of everything creativity has to offer.

ENOUGH

IN 2006, AFTER MONTHS OF DEBILITATING FATIGUE and vertigo, I was diagnosed with multiple sclerosis. I was sick and tired of being sick and tired. My attempt to do more, own more, and convince people that I was more didn't resonate with my heart and literally broke my body. All the excess that contributed to a stressful life may not have caused my disease, but it did exacerbate the symptoms. After my diagnosis, I turned my focus to eliminating stress. Not managing it, or reducing it, but getting it out of my life. It was killing me and my relationships.

I began to edit out unhealthy food, debt, clutter, toxic relationships, work I didn't love, and, eventually, a wardrobe that was always reminding me that what I had would never be enough. I used to have big collections of purses and sunglasses. When I pared down to one, people were concerned. Sounds silly, right? They asked me, "What will you do if you lose it or if something breaks?" Well, if and when that happens, I'll replace it or go without. I refuse to live in fear of not having enough.

What's enough for you, and what does your "enough is enough, things have to change" moment look like? Some people call it a wake-up call. Yours may have already come and gone several times, but it's never too late to answer the call.

Pre–Project 333, I had no concept of what "enough" meant to me. I was always focused on more. Instead of living an "enough is enough" life, I was more in line with "too much of everything is just enough." But eventually, the too much was too heavy. I started Project 333 for a few reasons, and one of them was to determine what enough meant to me. I didn't know. I was shocked (and delighted) to discover that in many cases, one was enough. I only need one pair of sunglasses, one purse, one pair of jeans, and one winter jacket. This is a stark contrast to my former collections of those items. One suits my needs, and when there is only one, I take better care of it and appreciate it more. Not to mention that I have no decisions to make in terms of which one to use on a day-to-day basis. I simply use the one I have. I've applied my "one is enough" philosophy to other objects, too. It doesn't work for everything, like pens and teaspoons—for some reason, I require more of these two things.

I'll never tell you what to include in your capsule wardrobe, but I highly recommend that you exclude the following, because seriously . . . enough is enough.

We've all had enough of:

1. PERFECTIONISM. You might not get your capsule wardrobe right the first time around, and chances

are, at the end of three months, you'll see everything differently. Don't worry about doing it right. This is a challenge, an experiment. And in three months, you can do it all over again.

2. COMPARISON. My wardrobe won't look like your wardrobe. You don't have to wear all black or own a dress you can wear five different ways. You live in a different climate, have a different lifestyle, and have different tastes in clothes. Make this project your own. If you follow #project333 on Instagram, you'll see that this is not a one-size-fits-all challenge.

3. STUBBORNNESS. If you get started and the shoes you included aren't working, swap them out. Just because you wrote your list on paper doesn't mean it's set in stone. Be fierce but flexible.

4. GUILT. When you're boxing up your clothes, you might feel guilty for spending too much on things you don't wear. What you should be feeling is proud that you are open to change. You should be feeling excited about a new challenge. Feel happy that your clothes may be going to someone who really needs them. Trade your guilt for the good stuff.

5. SUFFERING. If you wear out your favorite pair of jeans, or a coat that you included becomes a little too snug, replace it. If you're unhappy with your selection, reselect. Use Project 333 as a way to learn about what you really need and want in your closet instead

of treating it like a punishment. This should be fun
and make your life easier. If you're suffering or
struggling, change something or ask for help.

Leave those things out and make room for compassion,
grace, laughter, and lessons.

PROJECT 333 MIGHT BE MORE THAN ENOUGH

Joshua Becker, author of *The More of Less* and *The Minimalist
Home*, revealed how much "enough" Project 333 really is on his
blog, becomingminimalist.com. After recommending Project
333, a woman named Pamela shared some compelling information with Joshua:

Pamela Mullins is a teacher and piano instructor in North
Carolina. Recently, she accepted the Project 333 Fashion
Challenge and emailed me a list of her 33 items. Her son,
Eric, is a principal software architect with a mind for
mathematics. Pamela decided to include him in the
challenge by sending over her list of 33 items and a specific
breakdown mentioning which items could be worn together.
Based on that information, Eric created a mathematical
model to determine how many unique outfits she could wear
with the 33 articles of clothing.

His conclusion? **25,176 unique combinations.** That is
25,176 different outfits from only 33 articles of clothing. To
put that into perspective, Pamela could wear a different

outfit every day for the next sixty-nine years without ever repeating the exact same combination of clothes.

I found the number almost too unbelievable to be true. So I asked Eric to share how he reached that conclusion. The math looks like this:

Pamela's list of 33 items for Project 333:

1. jean jacket
2. black boyfriend jacket
3. long black pants
4. black capris
5. jeans
6. dress
7. black skirt
8. pink print skirt
9. denim shirt
10. checked shirt
11. elephant shirt
12. white shirt
13. cream/black print T-shirt
14. black three-quarter-sleeved slight-V-neck T-shirt
15. paisley blouse
16. polka-dot blouse
17. blue sweater
18. black scarf
19. floral scarf in blues and reds

20. black-and-white scarf
21. long necklace
22. bicycle necklace
23. flower necklace
24. fake diamond earrings
    (but you would
    never know the
    difference)
25. silver drop earrings
26. red music note earrings
27. silver bracelet
28. silver bracelet
29. black wedges
30. black sandals
31. black flip-flops
32. black closed-toe shoes
33. purse

Eric took every article of clothing, multiplied out the number of outfit configurations for each, and added them together:

- Never changes: **1 purse, 2 silver bracelets**—only one configuration.
- Can go with every configuration: **4 shoes**—top level (baseline).

MODEL DRESS: 4 (baseline) × 2 (black jacket or no jacket) × 3 (earrings or none) × 3 (necklaces or none) = 72

MODEL PINK FLORAL SKIRT: 4 (baseline) × 3 (jacket + sweater + none) × 1 (camisole) × 3 (earrings or none) × 4 (necklace or none) = 144

- Can go with every other configuration: **4 bottoms × 4 shoes × 4 (2 jackets, sweater, none)** = 64 new baseline

MODEL JEAN SHIRT: 64 (baseline) × 5 (shirt + T-shirts + camisole) × 4 (earrings or none) × 4 (necklace or none) × 3 (scarves or none) = 15,360

MODEL WHITE SHIRT: 64 (baseline) × 4 (earrings or none) × 3 (2 necklaces or none) × 3 (scarves or none) = 2,304

MODEL ELEPHANT SHIRT: 64 (baseline) × 4 (earrings or none) × 2 (1 necklace or none) = 512

MODEL BLACK CHECKED SHIRT: 64 (baseline) × 4 (earrings or none) × 2 (1 necklace or none) = 512

MODEL BLOUSES: 64 (baseline) × 2 (blouses) × 4 (earrings or none) × 4 (necklace or none) = 2,048

MODEL BLACK KNIT SHIRT: 64 (baseline) × 4 (earrings or none) × 3 (scarves or none) = 768

MODEL CREAM KNIT SHIRT: 64 (baseline) × 3 (2 earrings or none) × 2 (1 necklace or none) × 3 (scarves or none) = 1,152

MODEL STRIPED KNIT SHIRT: 64 (baseline) × 3 (2 earrings or none) × 4 (3 necklaces or none) × 3 (scarves or none) = 2,304

72 + 144 + 15,360 + 2,304 + 512 + 512 + 2,048 + 768 + 1,152 + 2,304 = **25,176 outfit combinations.**

It should be noted that some of the configurations contain very minor changes (with earrings or without earrings, for example). But still, a different outfit combination every day for the next sixty-nine years is pretty unbelievable—and accomplished with only 33 different articles of clothing.

There's a reason Project 333 is such a popular experiment in owning less. Most people who try it discover there are numerous benefits to owning fewer articles of clothing. And many people discover 33 is more than enough—including Pamela, who recently wrote this about her experience: "I actually love the simplicity and feel I have more than enough to wear."

FAST

USUALLY, WHEN WE THINK OF FASTING, WE THINK about food. Project 333 is a shopping fast and a fashion fast in the sense that for three months you are giving up shopping and thinking about all things shopping and fashion. Like any fast, you get to approach it in the spirit of sacrifice or freedom. It's your choice. Often, letting go is liberating. You now have one less category of stuff to think about. And there are zero decisions to be made when you're in a store. I remember grocery shopping at supermarkets that also offered clothing and accessories. A new scarf or pair of earrings always ended up in my cart and became part of my grocery budget. Letting that go was freeing. Simply taking the option off the table was so much easier than trying to manage the decisions around shopping, especially when I didn't really need anything new. I've heard similar stories from people who give up alcohol. Letting go of all the decision-making—"should I have one more, should I drink today, what should I drink, how much is too much"—feels good, even though they are giving up something they enjoy on some level.

Even though the focus of Project 333 isn't a shopping fast, fasting *is* part of it. Decide what to wear for the next three months, and that's it. At the end of the three months, if you decide to continue with 33 items seasonally, you'll have this freedom every season. It makes for much more intentional purchases and spending. You'll better understand why you buy, and once you're really thinking about it, it becomes challenging to buy things you don't really need.

HOW TO FAST FROM SHOPPING

When you quit shopping for a while, it may be easy enough to just call a full stop, but shifting your mind-set with these suggestions will help you change your shopping habits long after your fast is over.

CULTIVATE A MUSEUM MENTALITY. Living more simply doesn't mean you don't want more. The desire for more dissipates, but in my experience, it doesn't go away completely. Instead of finding gratification in the owning, find it in your appreciation for the item. For instance, when you walk through a museum, you can fully appreciate the art without owning it. The same goes for new clothing, gadgets, and other things. When you desire something new in your wardrobe, admire. Don't acquire.

WAIT AND SEE. That thing you *must* own will still be available next month. Wait thirty days before making any purchase and see if the item is still as necessary or appealing. I've saved so much money with the wait-and-see approach. I usually forget all about my seemingly must-have item within a few days.

SPEND IT ON PAPER. Carry a small notebook with you, and whenever you think about buying something, write down what it is and how much it costs. Do this for thirty days and see how much money you've saved. If you want to take this a step further, set the cash aside for every purchase you don't make. At the end of thirty days, you'll have a good contribution to put toward debt or to send to your favorite charity.

ESTABLISH GIFT POLICIES. Talk to your friends and family and come up with a way to reduce gift purchasing. Some people will be relieved to stop exchanging gifts, and others may be completely closed to the idea. For the most part, people will fall in the middle in the interest of preserving tradition. They may consider a new twist like gifting experiences over stuff or spending money on a dinner or weekend getaway in lieu of gifts. If you're ready to call off all gift giving, be gentle with people who aren't there yet, but hold your ground.

UNSUBSCRIBE. Unsubscribe from digital updates from your favorite retailers. Opt out of catalog mailings and stop reading sales flyers, if you haven't already. You won't miss what you don't know about. Pro-tip: If you have Gmail, make sure your Promotions tab is set up. Most sales emails will land there. Once a week you can select all and delete. If you see an email in your Promotions tab that doesn't belong there, simply drag it to your Primary inbox.

THE BUDDY SYSTEM. If you have shopaholic tendencies, team up with a friend or family member who likes to shop, too. Whenever you're about to make an impulse purchase, call your friend and talk through it. Do you need it? Do you need it today? Ask questions and be supported and supportive. We all need a little help sometimes.

REMOVE YOUR EMOTIONAL EXPECTATIONS. Your stuff does not have the power to change your life. Nothing you buy will make you a better person. Only you can do that.

SLOW

IN *HOW TO LIVE A GOOD LIFE*, AUTHOR JONATHAN FIELDS SAYS, "Fast and busy is a choice," and I have to agree. Our lives are fast and busy, but didn't we make them that way? And if we did, can't we make them slow and enjoyable? A full life doesn't have to be a run-yourself-into-the-ground, crazy-busy life. Life itself moves fast enough. It's up to us to create small pockets of slow into our days and weeks so we get a chance to notice our lives, to witness the smallest moments, and of course to enjoy this short time we have. Changing from fast fashion to slow fashion with Project 333 is one good way to start.

There is so much we can't control about how fast things are moving, so it's even more important to slow down the spaces and places we can. Simplifying things will help. Eliminating things will help. Less will help.

Here are a few areas you may be able to slow . . .

SLOW DOWN YOUR CLOSET. You knew I'd start here, right? Project 333 will naturally slow down your closet. Use what you learn to be even more intentional about future purchases and how you get ready for each day.

SLOW DOWN YOUR MORNINGS. Wake up a little earlier so you can savor your tea or coffee. Sit quietly and daydream. If your home is chaotic in the morning, see if there is anything you can do the night before to slow things down.

SLOW DOWN YOUR TABLE. If it takes longer to make dinner than to eat and enjoy it, it's time for a mealtime slowdown. Enjoy your food, reflect on your day, and connect with your people before you scrape your plates and rush off to your favorite TV show. Create

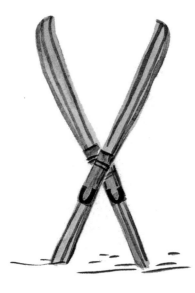

linger-y mealtime traditions to encourage a slowdown. For instance, on ski days, we leave the dirty breakfast dishes in the sink. The mountains are calling and we must go!

SLOW DOWN YOUR DIGITAL CONSUMPTION. Disconnect from your digital devices. Set limits for yourself. It's hard to break away. I get it. The internet is amazing and has so much to offer, but so does your life.

SLOW DOWN YOUR REACTIONS. Overreacting typically comes from a place of being overwhelmed. Simplicity invites you to underreact. Take time with your thoughts and words. You'll eliminate unnecessary stress and drama.

SLOW DOWN YOUR WORK. Sometimes people assume that because I work for myself, I have the luxury of working at a slower pace than people working in a more traditional setting. I may have more flexibility with my schedule now, but my slowdown began while I was working in a fast-paced sales job. I started my slowdown by checking email less frequently and leaving my work behind at the end of the day instead of carrying it into my evenings and early mornings. No one noticed, and I wasn't less productive. Fast and busy doesn't always result in good work, but it can lead to more mistakes and burnout.

Some stages of life will be more hectic than others, but you can still apply a slowdown filter just by the way you move through the day. You get to choose. Rush, stress, and hurry everyone along, or pause, smile, and take your time. Some things won't get done. That's okay. You won't look back and remember the time you didn't complete your to-do list, but you may look back and remember the beautiful life you lived.

CONFIDENCE

It's hard to admit, but I really did do the whole "dress to impress" thing. What I wanted to wear, or thought was appropriate, was secondary to what I thought other people expected from me, or what I thought would impress others, or what I thought would make people think I was convincing in the role I was playing. By doing this fashion challenge, I realized that real confidence couldn't come from the outside, and I began to find confidence in who I was instead of what I wore. I always thought I needed something new to wear to be confident. I needed the right heels to feel powerful, or a new dress to feel sexy, or a new jacket to feel put together and prepared. Doing Project 333, I feel all those things and more without anything new. Don't be confident in what you wear—be confident in who you are.

Dressing with less will help. If you don't have the confidence to start Project 333 right now, create it. Create confidence by taking tiny steps toward your tiny wardrobe.

Try one of these tiny steps:

1. **BOX UP EVERYTHING THAT DOESN'T FIT YOU RIGHT NOW.**
   You don't have to give it away—just get it out of your
   closet. You aren't wearing those clothes anyway, so
   why face questions about why they don't fit, why you
   bought them in the first place, or why change isn't
   happening as fast as you'd like. Eliminate the
   physical clutter, and the mental clutter goes
   with it.

2. **DONATE ANYTHING YOU HAVEN'T WORN IN FIVE YEARS.** I
   understand the arguments about not tossing stuff
   after a few months of not wearing it, but a few years?
   There's a reason you haven't worn that thing in years.
   Let go.

3. **UNSUBSCRIBE FROM ALL SHOPPING SITES AND STORES.**
   They will pull you in. It's their job. Don't put yourself
   in a position to have to push back. Instead, just
   remove the temptation—the sales, points, updates, all
   of it—from your inbox and your brain.

4. **IDENTIFY YOUR WEAKNESS.** Do you have more scarves
   than you could wear in a month? Too many pairs of
   shoes? When I told my sister about Project 333 for
   the first time, she said, "If I do it, I'll have one pair of
   jeans, a T-shirt, and thirty-one purses." She knows
   her weakness. Luckily, she's also still optimistic!
   Recently she told me this book might be the answer
   to finally getting her closet in order. (Alyson, if you

still need help after you read the book, you know where to find me.)

5. WATCH INSPIRING DOCUMENTARIES. If you want extra motivation to shop less, or to shop more thoughtfully, watch *The True Cost*, a powerful documentary about what it really costs to make your clothes. And take a look inside my closet and watch how others use minimalism to create meaning in their lives in *Minimalism: A Documentary About the Important Things*.

6. CURATE VISUAL INSPIRATION. Follow me on Instagram @bemorewithless and @project333, or search the socials for #project333. You'll find pictures of capsule wardrobes, daily outfits, and closets from all over the world.

7. PUT PROJECT 333 ON YOUR CALENDAR. Your tiny step is to simply put it on your calendar. If you're curious, revisit the rules in chapter eleven. Use the next few weeks to work slowly through the step-by-step process to whittle down your wardrobe to 33 items or less.

Again, this is not about the stuff. It's not even about the number of things you have. Dressing with less will help you discover so much more about your extraordinary life. Go without the excess in your closet for three months and see what it's really all about. Use these tiny steps to build confidence and then let the fashion challenge boost your confidence in the following ways:

- When you realize people don't notice you're doing the fashion challenge, you can stop stressing about what other people think overall.
- When you see that you're happier with less, and that 33 items are enough, you'll be more confident in letting go of things in your closet and other areas of your life.
- When you realize that even though you didn't prepare for every situation, everything is okay, you'll have more confidence moving through uncertainty.
- When you have some time to slow down and enjoy your morning, you'll feel more confident in how you move through your day.

Overall, taking on a challenge like this delivers a dose of confidence right from the beginning, because you were brave enough to try something new even though you may have been scared. You had the confidence to answer the question "Wouldn't it be crazy if . . ."

TRAVEL

TRAVELING IS A GREAT WAY TO SAMPLE A LIFE WITH less. It's when you're staying in a sparsely furnished hotel room or when you're far away from your own belongings that you realize not only how little you need to be happy but how you are more free, open, and present without the distraction of your stuff. I used to travel with more than I needed. Even for an overnight adventure, I'd bring a carry-on suitcase and a tote or large bag. And on longer trips, I'd check as many bags as I could. One time, on a trip to Sweden, one of my bags was lost. Even though the trip was fun, losing my stuff was such a distraction. I had to shop for new things and spend precious time chasing down a suitcase full of stuff. I stressed about what I needed, what I was missing, and how long it would take to reconnect with my very important stuff. Of course, none of it was important. I don't remember what was in that lost suitcase, and even though we recovered the suitcase, I doubt I still own any of its contents.

A few years ago, I began to experiment with traveling with

less. I took an overnight trip with just my laptop bag, a long weekend trip with only a small backpack, and a monthlong trip through several countries and climates with just a small carry-on bag. You can see what I brought here: https://bemorewithless .com/travel-2. After those ex-

periences/experiments, I'll never check a bag or bring anything extra when I travel again. I never want to wait in the lines required to check a bag, stand by a luggage carousel praying my bag arrives, or not be fully present for a trip because I'm chasing down lost luggage. My friends Eva and Leo Babauta of zenhabits.net take traveling light to the next level! They travel for weeks at a time with a 20L backpack each. To give you an idea of size, most children carry larger backpacks to school on a daily basis.

When I'm away for a night or two on a work trip, here's what I bring (weather dependent). I wear a black tee, jeans or leggings, a blazer, and flats, and in my laptop/workbag, I pack my . . .

- COMPUTER AND CHARGER
- PHONE AND CHARGER
- JOURNAL

- ID, CREDIT CARD, AND INSURANCE CARD
- EARBUDS
- PEN
- SMALL MAKEUP BAG
- HAIRBRUSH
- DRESS
- EXTRA SHIRT
- SLEEP SHIRT
- UNDERWEAR
- SUNGLASSES

I enjoy the freedom of moving through security lines with less. Navigating taxis or public transportation is much easier when you have less to carry and keep track of. A capsule wardrobe for overnights, weekends, and even three months at a time or longer simplifies everything so you can enjoy traveling through the world and life a little lighter.

PACKING

One thing that stresses people out about traveling is packing. I used to be one of those people. I eased my stress about packing by bringing everything with me. I was a chronic overpacker. And if the situation ever came up where I had packed everything and I still had a little space left in my suitcase, I felt like I'd won the lottery. More space equaled more stuff. I'd run around looking for other things that would fill the empty space. I might need that stuff. You know . . . just in case. One time I went to Mexico for less than a week. I brought five pairs of shoes plus the ones I was wearing, and then wore flip-flops for the entire trip.

I love to travel and see the world. Living with less has inspired me to travel with less, and vice versa. Everything I pack fits into a small carry-on suitcase and tote bag, or I don't bring it. That goes for a trip that lasts several days or several weeks. If you're planning a trip that requires different items than your Project 333 capsule collection, borrow them from your stored items. For instance, if you're going to the beach in the middle of winter, bring the appropriate items. If you love to travel, too, and want to see the world with a little less baggage, I hope you'll enjoy my best minimalist packing tips and resources.

PACK FOR HALF YOUR TRIP. If you're going to be away for a week, ask yourself what you need for three or four days. Don't be afraid to outfit repeat. People barely notice what you wear in your day-to-day life. It's unlikely anyone will notice or care while you travel.

CREATE PACKING LISTS. Before your next trip, list everything you bring with you. Check each thing off when you use it. At the end of the trip, you'll know you can leave anything home that wasn't crossed off on that type of trip. Keep your list handy, with details about where you went and what time of year it was, and save it so that the next time you take a similar trip, you'll know exactly what to pack.

UNDERSTAND YOUR LAUNDRY OPPORTUNITIES. Will you be staying somewhere with a washing machine? I'll rent an apartment from Airbnb specifically because it has a washing machine if I'm staying somewhere for longer than two or three days. Some hotels have laundry rooms for guests. At the very least, you'll likely have access to laundromats or your bathroom sink, where you can wash and line-dry certain items.

KNOW WHEN TO FOLD 'EM. I've tried rolling, stacking, and folding my clothes for packing and haven't noticed a big space difference. Hitha Palepu, author of *How to Pack*, says, "I roll my bottoms and fold my tops—I find my clothes end up with fewer wrinkles and I can fit more in my bag." The only way to really know what works best for you is to experiment. I recommend rolling your clothes for the first leg of your trip and then folding or stacking them on the return trip. See which method you prefer.

CREATE A TRAVEL-DAY UNIFORM. Assign one outfit for your travel day. Then you don't have to think about what to wear on the plane, train, or however you're traveling each time. No matter where you're going, your travel uniform can be the same. I typically wear black leggings, a short-sleeved shirt or tank top, and a black zip-up sweatshirt or blazer with a scarf (on or in my tote bag). I always bring a scarf! Even if I'm traveling to a warm destination, I know I'll get cold on the plane.

REMEMBER . . . "JUST IN CASE" MEANS "NEVER." When you notice you're adding items to your suitcase just in case you might need them, stop. Ask yourself why. Will you really use it, or do you feel compelled (like I was) to fill the empty space in your suitcase? Can you get it at your destination if you need it? What's the worst thing that will happen if you don't bring it?

DON'T FORGET WHAT MATTERS. If all your focus is on your stuff and what to pack, you may miss out on what really matters, like connecting with people on your travels or enjoying new locations. More important, don't forget about *you*. Take care of yourself while traveling.

Once you create your Project 333 collection, packing for trips will be so much easier. You could pack your entire wardrobe in your carry-on bag if you wanted to. Chances are, though, you'll want to move through the world with much less than that.

MORNINGS

Project 333 was that my mornings became easier. There was less rushing around, less stress, and much more of me showing up on time, present and ready to go, instead of feeling scattered and unprepared. Until all the excess was out of my closet, I didn't realize what a drain it was on my emotions and time while getting ready in the morning. Getting dressed is something we all do, so eliminating stress around that will naturally eliminate stress around your mornings. Think about how much more peaceful your mornings are on a day off, when you just throw on sweatpants or stay in your pajamas and take your time with a cup of tea or coffee. That's because you didn't have to think about what you were going to wear or make 4,000 decisions when you opened your closet. Project 333 has the same effect, but with actual clothes you can go do life in. It sounds so simple and logical, but because getting frustrated with our fashion decisions every day seems so normal, we keep doing it.

It was a rare day pre–Project 333 that I ended up wearing the first thing I tried on in the morning.

What happens in the first hour of your morning can dictate your mood and outlook on the rest of the day. For example, imagine yourself living the following two scenarios (both of which I've experienced).

MORNING #1

- WAKE UP AND HIT THE SNOOZE BUTTON (SEVERAL TIMES).
- FIND COFFEE.
- QUICK SHOWER DUE TO TOO MANY SNOOZE-BUTTON PUSHES.
- MUST FIND SOMETHING TO WEAR.
- OPEN CLOSET. SEE PLENTY OF OPTIONS.
- FIND NOTHING TO WEAR.
- TRY ON SEVERAL OUTFITS, STILL FEEL UNSATISFIED, BUT FINALLY PICK SOMETHING BECAUSE CLOTHES ARE NOT OPTIONAL TODAY.
- HEAD OUT, RUNNING LATE.

MORNING #2

- SET ALARM TEN MINUTES EARLY AND WAKE
  UP.
- START YOUR DAY WITH A MEANINGFUL
  MORNING ROUTINE.
- SHOWER.
- OPEN YOUR CLOSET AND SMILE AT YOUR
  MINIMALIST WARDROBE.
- GET DRESSED WITHOUT ANY COMPLICATED
  DECISION-MAKING.

Which sounds more enjoyable and less stressful? I've lived both mornings, and it's obvious the second choice creates the best possibility for an awesome day. When your morning goes well, there's a better chance that your day will go well. As author Annie Dillard says, "How we spend our days is how we spend our lives." The two best ways to create stress-free mornings that fuel a positive day are (1) create a small capsule wardrobe, eliminating the hassle of deciding what to wear; and (2) start a morning routine. Now that you won't be spending extra time getting ready, you'll have time for a morning routine. You'll have time to take care of you before taking care of everything else.

When you become more intentional about how you start your day, things begin to shift on the inside and the outside. This is what I call the morning routine effect. Here's what you can expect from the morning routine effect:

FOCUS. You'll feel less scattered and more focused all day long when you give yourself time first thing to settle in to the day. While it all contributes, the meditation component of my morning routine helps me come back more quickly during the day when I do get distracted.

CREATIVITY. Not only will you be more creative throughout the day, when you're practicing your morning routine with an open heart and mind, creative ideas seem to drop out of the sky. So much of my book- and blog-writing starts on the yoga mat or while journaling or walking in the morning.

PATIENCE. Learning to underreact is one of the best parts of the morning routine effect. You'll learn to pause, to consider your words, and to remember not to believe everything you think.

PRIORITY. A morning routine will help you understand what matters and, just as important, what doesn't. You can apply what you're learning to your to-do list, your day, and your life.

FUEL. A meaningful morning routine can fuel your heart, soul, body, and brain depending on the activities you choose. You can fuel up with food, too, by including a healthy breakfast at the end of your morning routine.

CONNECTION. Your morning routine will help you become more of the real you. The connection you're making with your own heart will encourage connections with the people you're meant to be with. The more you that you are, the more likely you are to attract the right people for you.

LIGHT. Your morning routine will add a sense of lightness to how you feel and how you see the world. If you practice your morning routine early, you may experience more sunrises, too. There's something magical about starting the day with the light of the rising sun.

HOW TO START A MORNING ROUTINE

Once you create your capsule wardrobe, come back here and use these steps to get your morning routine started.

1. **STOP SAYING YOU AREN'T A MORNING PERSON.** It's a great excuse, but it doesn't matter. Start your morning routine whenever your morning starts, even if it's in the afternoon.

2. **BE GRATEFUL.** Wake up and write down three things you are grateful for. If you can't think of anything,

remember what made you smile yesterday, the first person you thought of when you woke up, or the last thing that made you laugh.

3. STRETCH IN BED. Wiggle your toes. Roll your hips from side to side. Reach your fingers to the ceiling. Stretch your lungs, too, and take a few deep breaths.

4. HIDE YOUR PHONE. Do whatever it takes to be digital free until you've enjoyed your morning routine. Eventually you may want to use a meditation app or other tool on your phone during your morning routine, but start without it so you aren't tempted to check email, news, or social media.

5. MAKE A LIST OF MORNING ROUTINE ACTIVITIES. Eliminate the painful process of making decisions when you first wake up. Instead, make a list of what you'd like to include in your morning routine, and choose two or three things from it to start with.

6. CREATE A MORNING NOT-TO-DO LIST. You may have more clarity on how you want to spend your morning minutes after clearly identifying what you *don't* want to do or what's getting in the way of doing what you want to do. Make a list of the things that don't add value to your mornings. Craig Kulyk, founder of themorningeffect.com, recommends the following strategy for putting your morning not-to-do list into action:

Frame it by focusing on a positive habit you are prioritizing: Before I _____, I will _____.

EXAMPLES:

- BEFORE I CHECK SOCIAL MEDIA, I WILL STRETCH, MEDITATE, AND READ TEN PAGES.
- BEFORE I CHECK EMAIL, I WILL PLAN MY DAY.
- BEFORE I READ NEWS, I WILL EXERCISE, MAKE MY BED, AND WORK ON MY BUSINESS FOR ONE HOUR.

7. KEEP PEN AND PAPER NEARBY. Journaling is a great way to leave your worries on paper, work through an issue, or release some of the extra thoughts clouding your mind.

8. CREATE ACCOUNTABILITY. Challenge a friend to ten days of practicing a morning routine. Agree to text each other a simple "I did it" after your practice.

9. TURN ON MUSIC. Quiet background music can help to keep you engaged and present in your morning routine. Create a five-minute playlist (or grab the one from the Project 333 Resources page), and practice your morning routine for as long as the music lasts for the first week. Add a minute or two to your playlist and routine each week.

10. SHOW UP. Even if you don't do anything during your morning routine, show up for it every morning for a week. Dedicate five minutes to sitting on your

yoga mat, at your kitchen table, on the floor next to your bed, or wherever you'd like to be. Just show up.

If the only benefit of creating a capsule wardrobe is easier, more intentional mornings, it will be well worth it.

CHILDREN

SHOULD CHILDREN DO PROJECT 333? WHY NOT? IF YOUR
children are too young to pick out their own clothes, there are
still benefits to be had—namely for you. With fewer choices
and items to pick up and keep track of, you'll be less stressed.
Parenting can be stressful enough without anything extra. Just
like for you, 33 items may not be the right number for your
child, but experiment and see what works best. If it's causing
you more stress, it's the wrong number.

If well-meaning friends and family like to buy adorable outfits and donate clothes to your children, but you don't need
more clothes for them, have a gentle conversation about Project
333 and why you want to dress with less and dress your children
with less. If your children are old enough to decide what to
wear each day, tell them about Project 333 and include them in
the decision-making process. Remind them how cool it is to get
to wear your favorite things every day.

My daughter was a teenager when I started Project 333, and

while she knew about it, she wasn't interested in trying it. Many years later, she lived and traveled overseas for sixteen months with 33 items or less, and this prioritizing of experiences over things has translated into her life in powerful ways. Because I don't have experience with Project 333 and young children, I want to share some helpful tips from mom and writer Clare Devlin from simpleadventure.ca. Here is an example based on what Clare used for her daughters.

Items in each child's Project 333 wardrobe:

5 T-shirts

3 long-sleeved shirts

6 bottoms (shorts, pants)

2 light cardigans

3 heavier sweaters

2 dresses (or extra play clothes)

2 fancy dresses (or nice outfits for special occasions)

4 pairs of shoes (sneakers, sandals, dressy shoes, rubber boots)

1 hat

1 pair of sunglasses

1 jacket

1 pair of splash pants

1 bathing suit

1 backpack

When asked, "Does Project 333 really work for kids?" Clare said, "It can be difficult trying to stay on top of both the daily outfit changes and constantly changing sizes as kids grow. Therefore, the criteria for kids' capsule wardrobes might look different than it does for adults. For example, you might be less worried about style and investment pieces and more about what fits them and can be cleaned easily." Here are some criteria she recommends for choosing which pieces to use for your child's Project 333 wardrobe.

1. **MAKE A LAUNDRY SCHEDULE.** If you're worried that 33 items won't be enough, make a laundry schedule. This might seem like an odd step to begin with, but think about how often you do laundry and then work around this. For example, if you do laundry once a week, then you'll obviously need at least a week's worth of clothing.

   Thirty-three items will cover that many outfits, even with extra outfit changes during the day. If you find yourself doing laundry twice a week, you might get away with having less—or you'll have even more options!

2. KEEP TOPS AND BOTTOMS THAT MIX AND MATCH. If you have too much and are trying to pare down, I suggest keeping items that easily mix and match with one another. I do this by choosing pants that go with most of the tops: jeans, khakis, or colors that match a lot of existing items. That one mint-green butterfly-patterned outfit with pieces that specifically need to be together? Yeah, that's the one to go. When everything goes together, it makes it simple to grab a top and a bottom. And if you have kids who insist on dressing themselves, then you'll have the added bonus that they'll actually pick things that match.

3. STORE OFF-SEASON ITEMS. Eliminate the chaos of having everything in the closet or dresser at once. Only keep the items for this season, and then store and label any off-season clothes. I use a big Rubbermaid bin that sits on the top shelf in their closet. This also applies to any clothes that they will grow into soon. However, don't get carried away with storing for seasons; otherwise, this will become another source of clutter. Depending on the climate you live in, perhaps organizing twice per year could be enough: a spring/summer season and fall/winter season.

4. PASS ON CLOTHING. Other people might approach this differently, but I choose to give away clothes as soon as my children grow out of them. I'd rather give items

to someone who definitely needs it now than keep things for my own "someday, maybe." (The easiest time to go through clothes is when the seasons change, since you'll have to adjust their wardrobe then anyway.)

5. KEEP CLOSETS SIMPLE. I keep the kids' clothing in bins instead of in a dresser. Each child has one box for tops (T-shirts, cardigans, and sweaters), one box for bottoms (shorts, pants, and dresses), one box for underwear (including socks and a bathing suit), and one for pj's. Instead of hanging or folding clothes, I simply sort the clean clothes into the correct box. This makes it easy to put clean clothes away and easy to find things in the morning. When I move the boxes onto the floor, the kids can sort their own clean laundry!

This is great advice for adults, too! Follow Clare's advice if you want to try Project 333 with your children, and keep it age appropriate. Forcing a teenager into this fashion challenge may not end well for anyone, and overwhelming a toddler with all the rules won't work, either. Do what's best for you and your family and adjust as needed.

CONTAGIOUS

I love how it's trickled into every aspect of my life.
−PROJECT 333 TESTIMONIAL

THIS ONE SENTENCE SUMS UP THIS ENTIRE CHAPTER.
Project 333 won't just simplify your closet—it will trickle into every aspect of your life, and perhaps the lives of those around you. All the lessons I've learned from dressing with less encouraged me to live with less. They applied not only to my closet but to my kitchen, living room, garage, and beyond. From not only surviving but thriving with 33 items or less, I had the confidence to let go in every other area of my home and life. When you take on the challenge to dress with less, you'll challenge your relationship with stuff, your definition of enough, and what really makes you happy. This little fashion experiment is about so much more than clothes and hangers. It's about making the space, time, confidence, and clarity to create a life that is full of what matters most to you.

A SIMPLE CLOSET IS THE GATEWAY TO
A SIMPLE LIFE

When you discover the benefits of simplifying an area of your home that is part of your day-to-day life, like your closet, you get very curious about how simplicity may look in other areas of your home. If you're happier with only 33 items in your closet, you'll start to wonder if fewer wooden spoons, wire whisks, and pots and pans might make your kitchen experience a little better. Out of habit and preference, we generally wear the same things over and over again, and we use the same things in our home over and over again. The extra stuff just takes up space and other precious resources. Letting go creates a happier home and a calmer mind. We could all benefit from more happiness and calm in our homes and lives.

An article on Motherly (https://www.mother.ly/life/its-science-clutter-can-actually-give-you-anxiety) shares several scientific studies that demonstrate that clutter can actually increase anxiety. "Clutter can trigger the release of the stress hormone cortisol, which can increase tension and anxiety and lead to unhealthy habits." Scientific proof aside, think about how you feel when you walk into your home at the end of a full day. Imagine your phone starts buzzing, there's laundry spilling over the basket, and your kitchen table is covered with your kids' school papers and other odds and ends. Just that is anxiety-inducing. Between digital and physical clutter, we can feel overwhelmed by our surroundings.

Use the motivation from your capsule wardrobe to take the next step in reducing clutter in other areas of your home and life. Close the gap between inspiration and action, and take tiny steps each day. Thanks to taking tiny steps, I simplified my entire life and eliminated an enormous amount of stress. Check out these big changes I made and the tiny steps that made them happen.

BIG: Changed my diet

TIMELINE: 6 months to eliminate all the meat, and the rest of the changes continue to happen. I'll never stop experimenting with my diet because my body is always changing.

TINY:

- Read books about food and multiple sclerosis.
- Removed cows from my diet.
- Removed pigs from my diet.
- Removed chicken and other poultry.
- Removed fish and other seafood.
- Read books about vegetarianism to keep me motivated.
- Visited pigs and cows at local farms so I wouldn't want to eat them.
- Added more greens.
- Kept checking in with my body.
- Experimented with raw and vegan diets.
- Added more greens.
- Tried Whole30.
- Added fish and seafood.

- Cut out a ton of processed food.
- Eliminated most bread and pasta.
- Will keep checking in with my body.

> BIG: Paid off thousands of dollars in debt (like, tens of thousands)
>
> TIMELINE: 3.5 years to eliminate the debt
>
> TINY:

- Had gentle conversations with my husband.
- Started asking questions that started with "Wouldn't it be crazy if . . ."
- Listened to Dave Ramsey on the radio.
- Joined Financial Peace University (online).
- Saved $1,000 for an emergency fund (not all at once).
- Created a budget and spent every dollar on paper.
- Put any extra money toward our smallest debt.
- Let go of the guilt. I had already paid enough.
- Said no. A lot.
- Kept budgeting, having gentle conversations, and putting extra toward our smallest debts.
- Celebrated when we paid off our first card, first car, next card, loan, second car, student loan.

> BIG: Got rid of 90 percent of our stuff
>
> TIMELINE: 3 years to eliminate the majority of our stuff

TINY:

- Put a few things that I didn't care about in a box.
- Decluttered and removed the easy things (like duplicates, empty picture frames, shoes that hurt my feet).
- Noticed the space I created.
- Felt a little lighter.
- Decluttered and removed things that weren't as easy to let go of (like clothes I had spent a lot of money on, small appliances I never used, other decor, furniture).
- Noticed the space I created.
- Felt a little lighter.
- Decluttered the hidden clutter (the boxes in the garage and storage shed, things tucked on high shelves and under beds).
- Sold anything worth more than $50, gave away anything worth less than that.
- Turned to the harder items like books and sentimental items and let them go, too. Not all, but most.
- Noticed empty rooms in our house and was ready to let go of that, too.

BIG: Downsized from 2,000 square feet to 750

TIMELINE: We had our first serious conversation about selling the house in October 2012, listed the house in March 2013, and moved into our apartment in May 2013.

TINY:

- Asked my husband, "Wouldn't it be crazy if we sold our house and lived somewhere else?"
- Talked about the pros and cons.
- Met with a Realtor in December 2012.
- Hired someone to replace the carpeting.
- Painted the inside of the house ourselves (but should have hired someone).
- Removed the cats and dog any time there was a showing (ugh, I almost forgot about those afternoons).
- Discussed what mattered most to us and ignored advice to wait until "the market bounces back" before selling. Money wasn't driving our decision. There were more important things to consider, like how we wanted to live our lives.
- Moved into a 750-square-foot apartment with husband, daughter, big dog, and two cats.
- Celebrated our daughter's high school graduation a month later on the community rooftop deck overlooking the mountains.
- Knew we had made the right decision when my husband woke up one Saturday morning and said, "Guess what I'm not doing today? I'm not raking leaves, mowing the lawn, replacing the roof, or negotiating with neighbors to replace the fence." Instead, we went for a hike.

Your simplicity won't just be contagious from room to room in your home, but it could spread to other people, too. In my experience, trying to convince or get your family on board doesn't work, but inspiring them by walking the walk? That works. Remember how important the tiny steps are when you're picking your 33 items or making decisions about the other stuff in your home. Letting go, choosing less . . . it may matter more than you think.

LESS

LESS HAS LED TO MORE IN ALMOST EVERY AREA OF my life, in really meaningful ways. Living with less hasn't been a sacrifice but instead a journey in discovering what matters most. Here are a few ways I can promise you that living with less will lead to so much more.

1. **OWN LESS FOR MORE SPACE, LOVE, AND CONNECTION.** Our homes are not containers for stuff but rather a place for love and connection. By removing clutter from our homes, we make more physical space and create less distraction, allowing us to really live the way we want to live.

2. **DRESS WITH LESS FOR MORE TIME, MONEY, AND CLARITY.** If you've ever looked in your closet and thought, *I have nothing to wear*, while staring at hundreds of choices, I can promise you relief by dressing with less. Thanks

to Project 333, I spend less time and money shopping and experience less decision fatigue choosing from a small capsule collection.

3. DO LESS FOR MORE PRODUCTIVITY AND CREATIVITY. I accomplish more and do better work by doing less of it. You know how it feels to try to get something done when you're burned out from trying to do it all. Your work suffers. Your health suffers. Your people suffer. There will always be more to do. Choose less and do it well. Choose less and do what's most important.

4. LESS RUSHING LEADS TO MORE LINGERING. Lingering is like falling in love. Think about the evenings you've sat around a table after a meal, talking and laughing instead of rushing to clean up the dishes. You fell in love with the people around you and the evening you shared. Likewise, lingering over a sunrise, a good book, a long walk, or a moment of solitude encourages love: love of what you are experiencing, love of who you are spending time with, and love of who you are.

5. WORRY LESS FOR MORE PEACE AND SLEEP. Worry keeps us up at night. Worry weighs us down. Worry encourages fear and makes us tired, cranky, and scared. But here's the thing: How much we worry about something never determines its outcome. Worry is a trap. Simplicity helps you worry less.

With less around, there is less worry. Be discerning about what you choose to surround yourself with. Hold on to what matters. Let go of the rest.

6. **SAY YES LESS FOR MORE TIME TO DO THINGS YOU LOVE WITH PEOPLE YOU LOVE.** We've all said yes when we wanted to say no. Whether we say it out of guilt, fear of missing out, or habit, it's important to note that saying yes when your heart says no is a disservice not only to you but to everyone you say yes to. If your heart says no, it will fight the yes all the way through. You won't be excited to contribute. You won't give your best, and you may end up resenting the commitment or the person who asked you to make it. If you don't have time for what matters, stop doing things that don't.

7. **CONNECT LESS TO YOUR DIGITAL DEVICES FOR MORE CONNECTION WITH WHO YOU ARE AND WHAT YOU KNOW TO BE TRUE.** If you want real connection and honest answers, check your heart more than you check your phone. Start by sitting quietly for a few minutes with your hands on your heart and your eyes closed. Listen to your heart. She knows things.

8. **LESS DRAMA RESULTS IN MORE EASE AND EQUANIMITY.** Choose to underreact. Choose to take a few (hundred) deep breaths. Choose a long walk. Don't let the drama in.

There are some surprising things about living and dressing with less, too. I expected to save money and create space, but here are a few benefits I didn't expect:

FRIENDLINESS. When you reduce stress and free up time and space, you can naturally give more thought to how you treat people and how you react in different situations. You can take the time to give more compliments, listen carefully, and smile more. Living and dressing with less may make you a nicer person.

SILENCE IS MORE APPEALING. In a high-pressure lifestyle, you may think you thrive on stress and speed, but once you pull back, you'll come to appreciate silence and solitude.

LIVE A HEALTHIER LIFESTYLE. Listening to what your body really needs is so important, but how can you hear the messages amid constant chaos? Creating a simpler life gives you time to pay attention, make changes, and do what you need to do to live a healthier lifestyle.

YOU CAN BUY WHEN YOU'RE READY. Advertisers want to convince you that you need the latest and greatest. Then they create sales and specials to remind you that you need it now. When you want and need less, you can buy what you need when you're ready, not when they are ready. That eliminates all concern for billboards, pop-ups, coupons, sales, rewards programs, and other silly distractions.

SIMPLE IS SEXY. Minimalism says, "This is who I am without all the stuff." It says, "I'm removing the layers of excess so I can know the real me and you can know the real me." That's sexy.

YOU CAN BE OPEN TO UNCERTAINTY. Minimalism provides room for uncertainty. When you live with less, you move through the world with a lightness that allows for change and the uncertain nature of life. When you aren't weighed down with stress, stuff, and worry, it's easier to let go, make simple shifts, and transition with grace.

For some of us (like me), it takes years of tiny steps to simplify your life, but we get to experience the benefits of less along the way. Living with less has helped me to restore my health, engage in work I truly care about, and show all the way up for the people I love. Living with less can lead to so much more.

LOVE

IF YOU READ MY FIRST BOOK, *SOULFUL SIMPLICITY*, OR HAVE read anything on bemorewithless.com, it will not be a surprise to you that there is a chapter about love in a book about a fashion challenge. After all, we don't simplify our lives and clean out our closets only for the sake of clean countertops and pretty closet space. I mean, those things are nice, but they aren't sustainable if we don't have other reasons to stay simple. Reasons like peace, ease, and, most important, love are what keep us engaged in simplifying our lives. Whether we start in our closets or kitchen drawers, or in our careers or calendars, what we want is more time and space for who we love and what we love. We want room for more love in our lives, which means less stuff, busyness, debt, and stress.

Now, if you're shaking your head and thinking, *But what I love is shopping, clothes, and fashion*, it's possible that you haven't taken the time or don't have the time, space, or energy to figure out what you really love. I don't say that to be critical. In fact, I used to think the same thing. I used to love shopping and clothes and shoes and sparkly things, too, or at least I thought I did, so I may have something to offer here. The truth is that I didn't really know what I loved. Maybe you don't know what you love, either. Perhaps, because so much of your attention goes toward the things in your closet, you've confused that for love. But what do you really love? What makes your heart sing? What would you rather be doing? Where would you rather be? What are you actually curious about and interested in? Don't worry if you don't have answers to those questions, or if you haven't even ever considered them. Many of us never do. We are so busy doing all the things we're supposed to be doing and paying attention to what we thought we were supposed to be paying attention to (not to mention that we're overwhelmed, exhausted, distracted, and stressed out with our heavy, busy lives) that perhaps we forgot we had some choices here. Maybe we forgot we could break the rules, write new rules, care about something other than getting dressed in the right clothes and buying new crap. It's easy to love shoes and dresses, but that's not deep-down, heartburning, upside-down, mildly obsessive, seeing-stars love. If you want to know what you love, or learn what you love, try this . . .

ASK THE QUESTION "IS THIS LOVE?"

At first I didn't understand how my "stuff" was getting in the way of love. I didn't see the connection, but my clutter, debt, and busyness were a big obstacle to living a life full of love. When the stuff was gone, I had space to consider what I loved. When the debt was gone, I had more freedom to explore work I loved. When the busyness was gone, I had the honor of being present and showing up for my life. I still want things or think I need something new from time to time, but now that I clearly see how my stuff was standing in the way of love, new stuff isn't as appealing. It's easy to walk away. Understanding how damaging my stuff really was wasn't an overnight revelation. It took me years to figure it out. If you're in the beginning stages of simplifying your life, or if you struggle when it comes to paring down or saying no, consider this one question before your next purchase or commitment . . .

Is this love?

Does this contribute to your life in a loving way, or support people you love, work you love, or something in your life you really care about? Does this thing help you live a life you love or encourage you to be more loving? Ask yourself if you're adding this thing, event, or commitment because it adds value or because it distracts you from pain: the pain of boredom, frustration, or uncertainty. Is there a better way to ease the pain?

Keep coming back to this question: *Is this love?*

NOTICE LOVE. LOOK AROUND AND CALL OUT LOVE WHEN YOU SEE IT.

When you read a book that pulls on your heartstrings, say, "This is love." When you hear someone speaking their truth, say, "This is love." When you see the top of a mountain, a sunrise, or a seedling popping through the dirt, say, "This is love."

The more you notice and name love, the more you will encourage it in your own life.

Simplicity is the way back to love. As you pare back and let go, you'll start to have more attention and energy to consider what you love. The most interesting observation I've made about the entire process, based on feedback from people who have dressed with 33 items or less, is that, in the end, this fashion project has very little to do with fashion or clothes and much more to do with health, happiness, and lots of heart. Like most everything that improves our lives and gives us a minute to consider who we are and what we want . . . this is love.

#PROJECT333

IF IT WEREN'T FOR THE PROJECT 333 COMMUNITY and their excitement, interest, support, and encouragement, this book would not exist. After a few years of writing about and sharing my Project 333 experience, I stopped. I thought I was done with it. I knew I'd still continue to dress with 33 items or less, but I wasn't going to write about it anymore.

Even after I stopped, I'd receive an email almost daily from someone with a question about Project 333, or someone expressing gratitude for the challenge. I took the Project 333 website down and closed the Facebook page, and people still kept the challenge alive by sharing their own experiences on blogs and social media. One day, when I was chatting with my friend Heidi from foodiecrush.com about our work, I told her I was going to give it up altogether. I can't remember exactly what she said in response, but it was something like, "Stop complaining. Project 333 is the way people find you on the internet. It's how they connect with your story, learn about simplicity, and change their lives." She was right, and since that conversation, I've continued to write about and share my Project 333 experiences and outfits, took my tiny wardrobe on tour, and wrote this book. It's something I never complain about or think about letting go of anymore because it's how we connect with each other. For some of you, it's your first step into a simpler life. If it weren't for Project 333, you and I might never have crossed paths. So all I can do is be grateful and say, "Welcome to the Project 333 community. I'm so glad you're here. Always let me know how I can be helpful."

The Tiny Wardrobe Tour started after I gave a talk at my friends Marc and Angel Chernoff's annual conference, Think Better, Live Better, about willpower. I mentioned Project 333, but it wasn't the focus of the talk. The next day, during a smaller Q&A meet-up, guess what every question was about? Project 333. That interest and Marc and Angel's support and encouragement inspired me to take my tiny wardrobe on tour. The first stop was New York City, and twenty-five people showed up. By the time I reached Toronto, we were selling hundreds of tickets. I brought my entire tiny wardrobe to each tour stop, but by the end of our time together, we were talking about stuff that matters way more than what was on the hangers behind me. If you'd like me to bring the Tiny Wardrobe Tour to your city, there's a request form on the Resources page.

I stay connected to the Project 333 community through email and social media, but mostly through #project333. Take what you've learned from this book and join us during any stage of creating your Project 333 tiny wardrobe.

How to join the community

1. Start the challenge.
2. Invite a friend.
3. Follow @project333 and @bemorewithless on Instagram and use #project333 and #bemorewithless on social media so I can cheer you on. Search #project333 on Instagram to connect with other people changing their lives by changing their closets.
4. Reach out and tell me about your experience.
5. Submit your #project333 story on the Project 333 Resources page for a feature on Instagram or other social media.

How to support the movement

1. Tell someone about it.
2. Review this book on Amazon.
3. Write an article on your blog or on medium.com about your experience (and share it with me, please).
4. Share your story with local media. I know it doesn't sound like breaking news, but chances are they will want to peek inside your closet.
5. Invite me to come and speak to your community.

Project 333 started as a personal closet challenge and grew into a worldwide community and movement to dress and live with less. If this were only about clothes and fashion, it would have been a passing fad. Instead, because the closet challenge affects so much more than closet space, it continues to spread and grow.

More Less

Everything you need to dress with less is in this book. If you want more less, head on over to https://bemorewithless.com/project333-resources, where you'll find helpful resources, including:

1. Project 333 Quick Start Guide, which you can use to make your capsule wardrobe list
2. Instagram Story templates to share your capsule wardrobe style
3. Playlists to help you clean out your closet
4. Invitations for free webinars and other live calls
5. Video and audio inspiration

If I didn't answer a question you have there, or in this book, please don't hesitate to ask me. Here are the best ways to get in touch: email courtney@bemorewithless.com, DM me on Instagram, or join one of the weekly live Instagram calls I host with my daughter, Bailey (@beautifuldetour).

Thank you for your brave, curious heart. I hope Project 333 changes your closet, and your life if you want it to.

xo,
Courtney

Acknowledgments

One of my favorite parts of writing books is thinking about the acknowledgments and how grateful I am for the people in my life. I've been sharing my simplicity journey and Project 333 for a decade. Without the following people, you might have never heard about me or Project 333.

Thank you to our like-hearted community; to everyone who has tried Project 333, used #project333, and shared their experience with friends or on their social media platforms and blogs in other ways. You got the word out. You made Project 333 a movement and a community instead of a fad. Thank you for sharing your stories and your hearts. I love you.

Thank you, Wendy Sherman. There are so many reasons I love that you are my literary agent, but the most important one is that you never shut down my ideas. You either love them, question them, or ask me to think differently about them. But you never shut me down. You only raise me up.

Thank you, Sara Carder. When I learned you were the editor for Julia Cameron's *The Artist's Way*, a book that made a profound difference in my life and work, I had little doubt that I wanted to work with you. I'm very grateful for your interest and attention and that you always make time for me when I'm in NYC.

Thank you to my TarcherPerigee team: Lindsay, Allyssa, Sara, Casey, Rachel, and the copy editors who make me look like I know what I'm doing when it comes to putting sentences together. I never want to write a book alone again.

Thank you, Joshua Fields Millburn, Ryan Nicodemus, and Matt

D'Avella for featuring my story and Project 333 in *Minimalism: A Documentary About the Important Things*. I loved spending time with you in Big Cottonwood Canyon and in my closet.

Thank you, Brett, Karl, Mike, Tatum Mike, Marc, and Angel, for masterminding with me, supporting me, laughing with me, creating with me, and most important, encouraging my decision to just foxing relax.

Thank you, Mark, for considering my crazy ideas and continuing to give me space to write, create, and heal. Thank you for all the beautiful places you take me to ski and hike. Even when I say I don't want to go because it's too cold, too hot, or too buggy, I'm always so glad I do (except for the time we hiked under the inchworm hatch). I'm looking forward to more adventures with you, my love.

Thank you, Bailey, for being you. You are all the good things. Thank you, too, for sharing thoughts on your blog, beautifuldetour .com and @beautifuldetour on Instagram. When I was your age, I didn't know what my own thoughts were, so I'm in awe that you share yours so beautifully. I'm also very grateful we work together. You are a big support for the Project 333 community and always inspire me to try new things on social media and to stay connected, especially when I want to hide sometimes. You will always be my best girl.

I'm very grateful for my friends who have become family and my family who became my friends. If it's true that we are the people we surround ourselves with, I am the very best person I can be.

© Mario Vega

Courtney Carver writes things. She wrote a book called *Soulful Simplicity* and the simplicity blog bemorewithless.com. She shares things that make her laugh and cry on Instagram (@bemorewith less). She doesn't know her Myers-Briggs Type, but she knows she's an introvert because she needs to be free from humans several times a day (cats and dogs are always welcome). Aside from her seasonal wardrobe, she doesn't count her things.

Carver doesn't have an impressive degree, awards, or a big, fancy home full of stuff. Instead, she selectively surrounds herself with her favorite things and the people she loves. She does work she truly cares about, goes on adventures (in the world or in her own backyard), and likes chai lattes with almond milk while reading or writing.

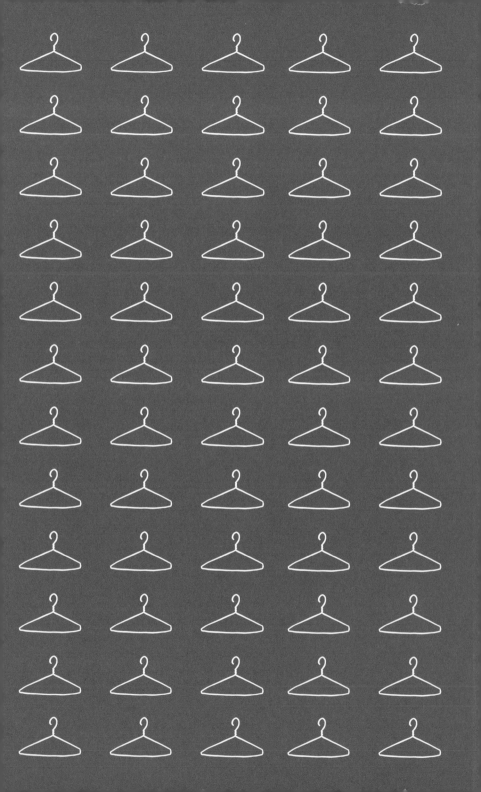